Dynamic Story Scripting with the ink Scripting Language

Create dialogue and procedural storytelling systems for Unity projects

Daniel Cox

BIRMINGHAM—MUMBAI

Dynamic Story Scripting with the ink Scripting Language

Copyright © 2021 Packt Publishing

Group Product Manager: Aaron Lazar
Publishing Product Manager: Harshal Gundetty
Senior Editor: Ruvika Rao
Content Development Editor: Urvi Shah
Technical Editor: Maran Fernandes
Copy Editor: Safis Editing
Project Coordinator: Deeksha Thakkar
Proofreader: Safis Editing
Indexer: Manju Arasan
Production Designer: Prashant Ghare

First published: October 2021
Production reference: 1061021

Published by Packt Publishing Ltd.
Livery Place
35 Livery Street
Birmingham
B3 2PB, UK.

ISBN 978-1-80181-932-9
www.packt.com

To the Inkle Discord and the larger ink community for supporting my previous work creating ink tutorials and video guides. To my friends, both local and remote, for being patient with me while I took on this project.

– Daniel Cox

Contributors

About the author

Daniel Cox is a PhD student in Texts and Technology program and a visiting instructor in the Games and Interactive Media department at the University of Central Florida with a decade of experience creating online learning materials across interactive fiction tools such as Twine, Bitsy, and ink. He previously helped create and served as the managing editor of the Twine Cookbook for 4 years. He currently teaches game design as a full-time instructor and volunteers with the Interactive Fiction Technology Foundation.

I want to thank the people who have supported me, especially my friends and my program advisor, Anastasia Salter.

About the reviewer

Johnnemann Nordhagen is an 18-year veteran of the game industry. He has worked as a QA tester, in Sony's Research and Development department, on the BioShock series at 2K Marin, and was cofounder of The Fullbright Company and the sole programmer on Gone Home. He founded Dim Bulb Games and headed the development of Where the Water Tastes Like Wine, released in February of 2018. He lives in Santa Fe, New Mexico.

Table of Contents

9
Story API – Observing and Reacting to Story Events

Section 3: Narrative Scripting with ink

10
Dialogue Systems with ink

11
Quest Tracking and Branching Narratives

12

Procedural Storytelling with ink

Assessments

Other Books You May Enjoy

Index

Preface

Dynamic Story Scripting with the ink Scripting Language teaches you an easy-to-learn narrative scripting language. Instead of needing to build an entirely new system for every project, ink allows authors to create story-driven content using a robust markup language designed for simple and advanced narrative experiences alike. Combined with the ink Unity Integration plugin, authors can work with developers to write all their story content in one language, ink, and access its variables, call functions, or move between sections of a story using code in Unity.

In this book, we will start with the ink itself. The first five chapters will walk you through how ink understands stories, manages the flow, the movement between sections of a story, and how to store and manipulate different values within a story. This will lead directly into the middle four chapters, which cover how to use the ink Unity Integration plugin and the application programming interface it provides to communicate between ink stories and Unity projects.

Finally, the last three chapters will highlight three common use cases. We will start with creating a dialogue system and review some approaches to handling data when using ink and Unity. Next, we examine how to create an advanced quest tracking system where each ink story contains a quest, but Unity is used to track values between them. The last use case will review some common terms and patterns across ink and Unity to help developers get started using procedural storytelling in their projects.

Who this book is for

This book is for Unity developers looking for a solution for narrative-driven projects and authors who want to create interactive story projects in Unity. Basic knowledge of Unity development and related concepts is needed to get the most out of this book.

What this book covers

Chapter 1, Text, Flow, Choices, and Weaves, describes the core concepts of ink, flow, choices, and the relationship between them.

Chapter 2, Knots, Diverts, and Looping Patterns, covers the divisions of stories, knots, and how to move between them.

Chapter 3, Sequences, Cycles, and Shuffling Text, explains programmable ways of generating dynamic text, alternatives, and their different forms.

Chapter 4, Variables, Lists, and Functions, covers how to store values in different ways along with advanced programming in ink.

Chapter 5, Tunnels and Threads, explains how to chain knots together, describes what tunnels are, and covers how to pull content into new configurations – threads.

Chapter 6, Adding and Working with the ink-Unity Integration Plugin, explains how to locate, install, and verify the installation of the ink-Unity Integration plugin.

Chapter 7, Unity API – Making Choices and Story Progression, covers how to select options in a weave and progress an ink story using the Story API in Unity.

Chapter 8, Story API – Accessing ink Variables and Functions, explains how to access and use ink variables and functions from Unity using the Story API.

Chapter 9, Story API – Observing and Reacting to Story Events, explains how to observe and react to changes in ink using the Story API in Unity.

Chapter 10, Dialogue Systems with ink, describes general approaches to creating a dialogue system in ink using hashtags, speech tags, and how the visual representation of options in Unity affects code in ink.

Chapter 11, Quest Tracking and Branching Narratives, provides a general template in ink for quests, how to track multiple quests from Unity, and an approach to synchronizing ink variables across stories.

Chapter 12, Procedural Storytelling with ink, provides an introduction to the term procedural storytelling, how to begin to use it in ink, and how the same approaches in ink work in Unity.

To get the most out of this book

You will need at least Unity 2021.1 and Inky 0.12.0. All code examples have been tested on Windows OS. However, they should work with future releases of both Unity and Inky.

Software/hardware covered in the book	Operating system requirements
ink 1.0	Windows, macOS, or Linux
Unity 2021.1	Windows, macOS, or Linux

Chapter 10, Chapter 11, and Chapter 12 include Unity projects. When using Unity projects from GitHub, remember to be patient as Unity rebuilds files when opening a project for the first time and to always open the SampleScene *scene in each project to see the final code.*

If you are using the digital version of this book, we advise you to type the code yourself or access the code from the book's GitHub repository (a link is available in the next section). Doing so will help you avoid any potential errors related to the copying and pasting of code.

Download the example code files

You can download the example code files for this book from GitHub at https://github.com/PacktPublishing/Dynamic-Story-Scripting-with-the-ink-Scripting-Language. If there's an update to the code, it will be updated in the GitHub repository.

We also have other code bundles from our rich catalog of books and videos available at https://github.com/PacktPublishing/. Check them out!

Download the color images

We also provide a PDF file that has color images of the screenshots and diagrams used in this book. You can download it here:

https://static.packt-cdn.com/downloads/9781801819329_ColorImages.pdf.

Conventions used

There are a number of text conventions used throughout this book.

Code in text: Indicates code words in text, database table names, folder names, filenames, file extensions, pathnames, dummy URLs, user input, and Twitter handles. Here is an example: "Every time the button is clicked, the Story method ChooseChoiceIndex() will be called with the correct index, and the LoadTextAndWeave() method will be called again, refreshing the value of currentLinesText and updating the current buttons shown on the screen... ."

A block of code is set as follows:

```
public class InkLoader : MonoBehaviour
{
```

```
    public TextAsset InkJSONAsset;


    // Start is called before the first frame update
    void Start()
    {
        Story exampleStory = new Story(InkJSONAsset.text);
    }
}
```

When we wish to draw your attention to a particular part of a code block, the relevant lines or items are set in bold:

```
void Start()
{
Story exampleStory = new Story(InkJSONAsset.text);
Debug.Log(exampleStory.Continue());
Debug.Log(exampleStory.Continue());
}
```

Bold: Indicates a new term, an important word, or words that you see on screen. For instance, words in menus or dialog boxes appear in **bold**. Here is an example:

1. Select the **Prefab** button in the project window.

2. In the **Inspector** view, click on the **Tag** drop-down menu and then click on the **Add Tag…** option.

> Tips or important notes
> Appear like this.

Get in touch

Feedback from our readers is always welcome.

General feedback: If you have questions about any aspect of this book, email us at customercare@packtpub.com and mention the book title in the subject of your message.

Errata: Although we have taken every care to ensure the accuracy of our content, mistakes do happen. If you have found a mistake in this book, we would be grateful if you would report this to us. Please visit www.packtpub.com/support/errata and fill in the form.

Piracy: If you come across any illegal copies of our works in any form on the internet, we would be grateful if you would provide us with the location address or website name. Please contact us at copyright@packt.com with a link to the material.

If you are interested in becoming an author: If there is a topic that you have expertise in and you are interested in either writing or contributing to a book, please visit authors.packtpub.com.

Share Your Thoughts

Once you've read *Dynamic Story Scripting with the ink Scripting Language*, we'd love to hear your thoughts! Scan the QR code below to go straight to the Amazon review page for this book and share your feedback.

https://packt.link/r/1-801-81932-7

Your review is important to us and the tech community and will help us make sure we're delivering excellent quality content.

Section 1: ink Language Basics

By the time you've completed this section, you will be able to describe the major core language concepts and patterns of ink and how to use their syntax. This section contains the following chapters:

- *Chapter 1, Text, Flow, Choices, and Weaves*
- *Chapter 2, Knots, Diverts, and Looping Patterns*
- *Chapter 3, Sequences, Cycles, and Shuffling Text*
- *Chapter 4, Variables, Lists, and Functions*
- *Chapter 5, Tunnels and Threads*

1
Text, Flow, Choices, and Weaves

This chapter introduces the core concepts of nonlinear storytelling by examining branching narratives and how ink supports creating them. Building on these concepts, this chapter also reviews using lines, text within them, and how to combine them.

As a central element of creating nonlinear, interactive narratives in ink, choices are explained and how best to use them. Weaves and collections of choices are discussed within the context of when a large branching structure might be needed and how to collapse these weaves into simpler parts using gathering points.

In this chapter, we will cover the following main topics:

- Understanding branching narratives as a flow
- Creating choices and making weaves
- Disappearing and sticky choices

Technical requirements

The examples used in this chapter, in `*.ink` files, can be found online on GitHub: `https://github.com/PacktPublishing/Dynamic-Story-Scripting-with-the-ink-Scripting-Language/tree/main/Chapter1`.

Understanding branching narratives as a flow

When holding a physical book, a reader moves through a story by turning its pages. The movement between pages is also a movement through the story. What is experienced by the reader is called a **narrative**. The story is the packaging of its content into different parts called **pages**. The reader's narrative, however, is the experience of the story across those pages.

In a digital setting, there are no physical pages. The words of a story could be stored as part of a simple text file or bundled together in something more complex. Parts of a digital story, which are the pages in a physical book, can also be arranged much more easily, and the reader might experience them in different configurations, creating new narratives from the same story content.

Consider the following example, where each sentence is a part of a story:

```
The sun was shining in a clear blue sky.
Clouds rolled in and it began to rain.
The clouds cleared away and the sun emerged.
```

When taken in order from the first sentence to the last one, there is a story where the major parts are the sun shining, the clouds coming in, but then the clouds leaving and the sun shining again. However, what happens if the parts are rearranged?

Example 1:

```
The clouds cleared away and the sun emerged.
The sun was shining in a clear blue sky.
Clouds rolled in and it began to rain.
```

With a different ordering, a new narrative is created for the reader. In this version, the progression begins with the sun emerging and shining. Next, the clouds move in and it begins to rain. In either case, only three events are used, but their order affects the narrative experience of the reader.

Nonlinear storytelling

In the second example, the story still makes sense. This time, however, the events start with the clouds, move into the sun shining, and end with the clouds returning. The second example, in moving around the events, is an example of **nonlinear storytelling**, where the events or parts of a story are experienced in a new or different way than created or originally written. The progression is not linear from one part to another as created in the story, but a cohesive narrative is still created:

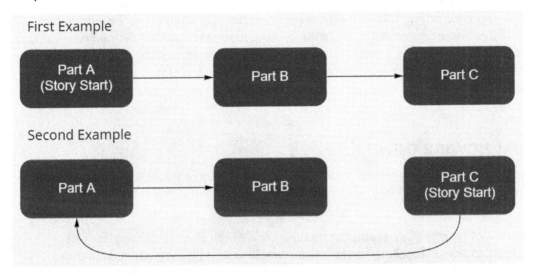

Figure 1.1 – Mapping nonlinear storytelling

The structures created by navigating a nonlinear story are often compared to *trees*. They start with a trunk and then, as different parts are encountered over others, a *branching pattern* is created, with each **branch** representing a movement through parts of a story from one end to another. The narrative traversal through a nonlinear story creates a *branching narrative*, where different parts were or were not encountered. The map of the experienced narrative represents a particular branch of the overall tree of the story and its parts.

While nonlinear storytelling can be done with a printed book, it is often much more difficult. In a digital setting, where events can be broken up into different parts, rearranging them can often be as easy as selecting them and dragging them to a different part of the same document. This consequence of representing stories as data makes writing code to handle arranging the different parts easier too. This is known as *narrative scripting*.

Introducing ink

ink is a *narrative scripting language*. It determines which part of the story comes next for the reader. As a user clicks or presses buttons, the code written in ink makes the decision between which branches they should visit and when. Based on rules written by an author, the code can even repeat the same part of the story with new values.

Because ink is designed for the purpose of scripting narratives, it understands navigation through a story as a special concept called **flow**. As the reader moves through the different parts, they are creating their own experienced narrative, which ink calls the flow. In fact, one of the most common errors encountered by authors is where the flow *runs out* of a story. Even when writing a nonlinear story with different branches, the story must start and end somewhere. Even if all the parts between the start and end of a narrative change each time a user traverses the parts of a story, these two points define the range of possible branches.

Text flowing down

The concept of flow also extends to how code is understood in ink. All movement across a story in ink moves *down from the top* of the code to the bottom unless told to navigate to a different part in the story.

The example stories shared earlier in this chapter are both also code examples. ink is designed to create branching narratives and supplies the ability to write code to create these structures. This means text or words written in a story without any other special characters or syntax are valid in ink.

Spacing within a line of text is important in ink. Because the text is considered a form of code, ink assumes any use of spacing is a deliberate choice on the part of the author. For example, adding extra spaces between words is not removed in its output:

```
The sun was        shining in a clear blue sky.
```

Output:

```
The sun was        shining in a clear blue sky.
```

ink ignores any empty lines. It assumes each line of text is important and any spacing between them should be ignored as something unimportant to the story itself.

Example 2:

```
The sun was shining in a clear blue sky.


Clouds rolled in and it began to rain.




The clouds cleared away and the sun emerged.
```

Output:

```
The sun was shining in a clear blue sky.
Clouds rolled in and it began to rain.
The clouds cleared away and the sun emerged.
```

The smallest unit is a line

The use of three lines as part of a story when introducing nonlinear storytelling was not a mistake. The smallest unit within an ink story is a single line:

```
This is a story.
```

Because ink considers text to be a part of the code, a single line with only four words is a completely valid story. Adding more lines would also extend what would be presented to the reader, but a single line can be a story by itself:

```
This is a story in ink.
It has two lines.
```

The use of the term *line* is important in ink. When reading a physical book, the smallest unit in a story is usually a sentence. This is often the smallest complete thought in a larger work. In a digital context, and specifically within ink, a line is the smallest unit. When ink loads a story, it moves through the story line by line. It treats each as equally important as the last.

As more complex code is introduced, the concept of a line will become more important as well. However, just like the single-line example, a story need not be complex to be important. To ink, a story is composed of lines. This could be one or potentially many more.

Gluing lines together

An author may need to use multiple lines of text as one "line" of code. For these situations, ink provides a concept called **glue**. When the less-than and greater-than symbols, < >, are used together, they glue the content of one onto the next, creating one long line:

Example 3:

```
This <>
is <>
considered <>
one <>
line of text.
```

Output:

```
This is considered one line of text.
```

Spacing when using glue is important. As with spacing within a single line, ink respects the choices of the author when presenting text in a single line. When using glue, these spaces are also respected.

Without the spaces after each word, the use of glue in the previous example would glue all the words together:

```
This<>
is<>
considered<>
one<>
line of text.
```

Output:

```
Thisisconsideredoneline of text.
```

Using comments as notes to authors

As a scripting language, ink also provides the ability to include notes within the code of a story. Borrowing from a more general programming term, ink calls these notes **comments**. They begin with two slashes and then contain the content of the comment. Any part of the line is also considered part of the comment:

Example 4:

```
The sun was shining in a clear blue sky.
// Change this next line in the future.
Clouds rolled in and it began to rain.
// Maybe update this story in a future version?
The clouds cleared away and the sun emerged.
```

When run, the text of the story would be treated as its code. However, any use of comments would not appear in the output of the story. Comments are only designed for human audiences and allow an author to explain the code to other audiences, or, more generally, as notes to themselves or other members of their team about how something works.

Working with Inky

To help authors more quickly develop a story in ink, **Inkle Studios** has created a program called **Inky**. This editing tool allows an author to write code and see it run as a preview of its output:

Untitled.ink

No issues.

End of story

Figure 1.2 – Screenshot of the Inky editor

While initially developed by Inkle Studios, Inky is now an open source project and often sees dozens of commits by the community to fix small issues or add new functionality. A new minor version usually comes out every year.

At the time of writing, Inky does not have a Windows installer but provides builds for macOS X and Linux systems. When running on Windows or Linux, the ZIP file needs to be unzipped to an existing folder and the `Inky.exe` (for Windows) or `Inky` (for Linux) file run to open the editor.

Using Inky

Inky presents an interface with two panes:

- The left is where ink code is written.

- The right shows a preview of the code while it is being developed.

This allows users to quickly see how their code would produce different outputs depending on what code was used.

Inky's most useful function is the ability to "rewind" a story to an earlier point and try a different branch of the narrative. This allows authors to test branches of their story more quickly, without needing to restart the story each time.

Figure 1.3 – The "Rewind a single choice" and "Restart story" buttons

> **Important note**
> This book will use screenshots from Inky to show the resulting output of different code.

Creating choices and making weaves

While having code pick parts of a story to produce a new possible narrative for a user could be exciting, most users want some input on what happens next. They want an interactive story. In ink, interactivity is created by presenting the user with choices. Depending on which choice the reader makes, the narrative could then branch in different ways.

Making weaves

Choices in ink are a part of another important concept, **weaves**. As a user creates a flow from one part to another, they often encounter intersections within a story where branches might be possible depending on what choice is made. This is what is known as a **weave** within ink. These are collections of choices where each one has the potential to branch the story in different ways.

Choices are written in ink using an asterisk, *. What might appear as a list of things is, in ink, each a different choice within a single weave:

```
What did I want to eat?


* Apples
* Oranges
* Pears
```

In the previous code, each line starting with an asterisk is a choice. It starts from the asterisk and extends to the end of the line. Everything that is part of the line becomes a part of the choice. Each asterisk on a new line creates a new choice within the weave:

```
We smiled again at each other across the coffee shop. I had
seen her coming in at this same time for over a week now. We
had spoken a couple of times, but I could not bring myself to
talk to her more.
As I looked back down at my coffee, I needed to decide.
* I decided to go talk to her.
"Uh. Hi!" I said, maybe a little too loud as I approached her.
* I gave up for now. Maybe tomorrow.
I shook my head to myself and looked away from her and out the
window. Today was not the day.
```

Each choice in a weave has the potential to branch the narrative. In the previous code, there are two choices. However, after each choice is another line of code. When run, ink would understand each line following a choice as being the result of choosing the reader. To help to visually differentiate the result of the choice better, the line following a choice is often indented at its start.

Changing the previous code to use indentation would look as follows:

Example 6:

```
We smiled at each other again across the coffee shop. I had
seen her coming in at this same time for over a week now. We
had spoken a couple of times, but I could not bring myself to
talk to her more.
As I looked back down at my coffee, I needed to decide.
* I decided to go talk to her.
    "Uh. Hi!" I said, maybe a little too loud, as I approached
        her.
* I gave up for now. Maybe tomorrow.
    I shook my head to myself and looked away from her and out
        the window. Today was not the day.
```

Choices within choices

Choices can also appear inside other choices. These are sub-choices and use an additional asterisk to indicate that they are the result of a previous layer of a weave:

Example 7:

```
Should I really forgive her again? I thought about the options
in front of me as I considered what she told me.
* I forgive her.
    ** She does the same behavior again.
        I just end up hurt again.
    ** She really does change.
        She does not have another affair and maybe we can save
            our relationship.
* I do not forgive her.
    ** I would have to move out.
        I would need to find another apartment.
    ** I stay with her and try to live again without being in a
        relationship.
        I could try going back to being friends like we were
            before our relationship.
```

In the previous code, there are two choices that each lead to their own choices, branching off the central set. This is an example of a **complex weave**. The first layer of the weave is the initial two choices. The result of either choice is then another weave, which then ends in text. Depending on the user's flow, they might only see part of the overall story when moving between these parts.

One possible branch within the complex weave could be the following output for the reader:

Output

```
Should I really forgive her again? I thought about the options
in front of me as I considered what she told me.

I forgive her.

She does the same behavior again.

I just end up hurt again.
```

A different series of branches within the story might also create the following output:

```
Should I really forgive her again? I thought about the options
in front of me as I considered what she told me.

I do not forgive her.

I would have to move out.

I would need to find another apartment.
```

Selective choice output

When using choices, the text of the choice itself appears in its output. This can be changed by using a special concept with choices called **selective output**. By using open and closing square brackets around any text in the line of the choice, it will not appear as part of the output as a result of making the choice:

```
What did I want to eat?


* [Apples]
* [Oranges]
* [Pears]


I got some food.
```

In the previous code, the output, regardless of the choice made by the reader, would be the same:

```
What did I want to eat?


I got some food.
```

In the cases where the text of the choice is different from what is shown to the reader, the term **option** is used. A choice is created in ink using code. What is ultimately shown to the reader is an *option*.

In more advanced code examples, ink can generate choices dynamically. In these cases, as with selective output, it can be important to understand the use of a choice as something written by a developer and an option as selected by the reader. Often, these can be the same thing, but they do not have to be when writing code in ink.

Selective output also allows creating more dynamic output by selectively showing text from an option in the output. An effect of using selective output is that the closing square bracket in a line signals an end to what is shown to the reader. Any additional text on the same line is ignored:

Example 8:

```
I looked at the timer again and then at the wires in front of
me. I had five seconds to stop this bomb from exploding.


* [I cut the wire.] It was the green one.
```

```
*  [I cut the wire.] It was the red one.
*  [I cut the wire.] It was the blue one.
```

Possible output:

```
I looked at the timer again and then at the wires in front me.
I had five seconds to stop this bomb from exploding.
```

```
It was the green one.
```

From the reader's perspective, the previous code would show three options. Each one would read I cut the wire. However, the use of selective output is telling ink to ignore the additional text of each color. After making a choice, the user would then see the result of the choice as a new line, with the use of square brackets excluding anything they enclose.

Selective output can often be useful to *hide* additional information behind a choice where the reader must pick an option and then see the additional text of a line.

Gathering points

Each choice in a weave can potentially branch a narrative. However, sometimes there is a need to gather one or more branches back to where they began. Instead of leading off in a new direction, a gathering point can be used to collapse a more complex weave into a *central point*. In ink, *gathering points* are created using a single minus sign (-) on a line:

```
You peer down at the desk with two drawers.


* Try to open the top drawer.
    It does not open.
    ** Try again more forcefully.
    ** Give up for now
* Try to open the side drawer.
    It does not open.
    ** Try again more forcefully.
    ** Give up for now
- All the drawers seem locked tight.
```

In the previous code, there are two choices with two sub-choices each. However, at the bottom of the weave is a *gathering point*. No matter what branch is taken across the first weave and then into the next layer, the flow will always gather at the last line. This is the power of gathering points: they allow a complex weave with multiple layers to collapse into a single point.

The placement of gathering points is important. In ink, stories flow down from the top to the bottom. If the gathering point appeared before the weave, it would be ignored. Without anything to gather, the gathering point does nothing. This also only affects weaves. Multiple gathering points in a story would do nothing without a weave *above* them to act as a point of collapsing them.

Gathering points only work on a single weave at a time. As the last line of a weave, they act to *gather* the choices. However, they only apply to one branching structure at a time. A new gathering point is needed per weave to collapse those branches back together:

Example 9:

```
You peer down at the desk with two drawers to open.

    * [Try the top drawer.]
    * [Try the side drawer.]
    - All the drawers seem locked tight.

You give up on the drawers and look at the top of the desk.

    * [Look at the papers on top of the desk.]
    * [Pick up the papers and look through them.]
    - You find nothing of interest.
```

In the previous code, both selective output and gathering points are used to create the illusion of two weaves with two choices each. The outcome of each, because they are using gathering points, is the last line of each. Options are presented to the reader, but the code itself collapses any possible branching of each weave and flows the story from the first weave to the second layer.

Disappearing and sticky choices

The default behavior of a weave is to direct the flow of a story along with one of the branches presented by its choices. When the reader makes a choice, the others *disappear*, and the branch chosen becomes the current flow of the story. Even when rewinding when using Inky to test a story, there appears to only be one valid branch of a weave at any one time.

Anticipating situations where the reader might revisit a part of a story with choices the reader might not have seen before, ink uses the concept of sticky choices to present the same choices again to the reader. Using sticky choices, each remains *open* during a revisit and can be used again in the future:

```
You look at the boulder in front of you.


+ Push the boulder.
```

Sticky choices are created using the plus sign (+). They can be thought of as the opposite of a gathering point. Instead of collapsing a weave, a sticky choice *keeps open* the option within a weave of using a different branch. Any sticky choice created as part of a weave is always *sticky*, even if it is the only one within the weave:

Example 10:

```
You look at the boulder in front of you.


+ Push the boulder.
* Ignore it for now.
```

In the previous code, there are two choices:

- The first is a sticky choice.

- The second would be removed upon a second visit to the code.

In the example, `boulder` could be ignored once, but the next time the reader visited the part again, they would only see one option: `Push the boulder`.

In examples where the story only flows down from top to bottom, sticky choices seem of little use. Upon making any choice, the story would flow along a branch and to the next lower part in the story regardless of the choice type:

```
The blank page stared back at me, taunting me. I glanced again
at the clock and then back at the page. I needed to write
something.


+ I tried again to write something.
    I wrote a few words and paused.
+ I checked my email again.
    No new messages.
```

In the preceding example, there is a single weave with two sticky choices. When moving through the story from top to bottom, the weave would be visited once and either choice would branch out and then back together again at the end.

The same example could be made with the other choice type.

Example 11:

```
The blank page stared back at me, taunting me. I glanced again
at the clock and then back at the page. I needed to write
something.


* I tried again to write something.
    I wrote a few words and paused.
* I checked my email again.
    No new messages.
```

Where the two code examples are different is in their intention. In the first, the reader could, potentially, revisit the same part of the story and see the choices again. In the second, the choices are one-way. By making a choice within the weave, they cannot be revisited in a story. Once made, a basic choice is permanent. The only way to change this intention is to use sticky choices that *add* themselves back to the weave when used.

In the next chapter, *Chapter 2, Knots, Diverts, and Looping Patterns*, we move into examining loops and controlling the flow of a story across more complex structures. Loops will allow us to revisit the same section of a story multiple times. In these cases, sticky choices will become the default usage for creating options for the player. Because sticky choices remain open, they allow an author to create a weave where a player can select the same option multiple times.

Summary

This chapter provided you with an explanation of the term story, content, and the narrative, what the reader might experience from its content. We examined nonlinear storytelling as how the parts of a story can be experienced in an order different than how they were written or originally composed. Next, we learned about branching narratives as a description of experiencing a nonlinear story where different sequences, branches, are explored over others. Through using code (scripting), we saw how different narratives can be created by controlling when the reader experiences story content.

ink is a narrative scripting language. We understand the movement through a story as a concept called flow. We discovered that each intersection, created by using different types of choices, is known as a weave. By using choices, we saw that different layers of a weave and more branching are possible. For situations where a weave is growing too complex, we can use a gathering point. This collapses a weave into a single point or line.

In the next chapter, we will begin to use knots, labeled sections of a story, and diverts, moving between these, to build on the concepts of nonlinear storytelling and branching narratives. We will start to use choices to move the reader to a particular knot or repeat the same weave again.

Questions

1. What is the difference between the story and the narrative?
2. How does ink understand the concept of flow?
3. How can multiple lines of text be combined into one?
4. What is a weave made of in ink?
5. What are the different types of choices?
6. How can selective output be used to hide information from the reader in a choice?
7. Why might a sticky choice be the preferred way to present options to the reader?

2

Knots, Diverts, and Looping Patterns

This chapter introduces the concept of knots, sections of an ink story, and diverts, which is the functionality to move between them. We will then move into defining and moving between knots to create simple looping patterns. By incorporating choices (covered in *Chapter 1*, *Text, Flow, Choices, and Weaves*), we will see how you can begin to experience narratives composed of selecting options, having the story move between knots, and then use looping patterns to build complex interactions from simple rules in ink.

In this chapter, we will to cover the following main topics:

- Tangling a flow in knots
- Moving between sections
- Looping knots
- Detecting and changing options

Technical requirements

The examples used in this chapter, in `*.ink` files, can be found online on GitHub at `https://github.com/PacktPublishing/Dynamic-Story-Scripting-with-the-ink-Scripting-Language/tree/main/Chapter2`.

Tangling a flow in knots

In *Chapter 1*, *Text, Flow, Choices, and Weaves*, choices were explained as capable of branching a story into different sections. Some simple branching structures were shown, but movement through a story consisted of flowing down from one weave to another. When a section is given a name in ink, it becomes one of its central concepts: a **knot**. A knot is a section of an ink story created by using at least two equals signs (==) and the name of the knot on a single line. After this definition, every line until the next knot encountered becomes a part of the original knot. By giving names to sections, they can be navigated to within ink to create more complex narrative experiences for readers.

Creating knots

A physical book is often divided into chapters. With knots, a digital ink story can also be divided into different parts. While a novel or textbook might use names for sections based on the word *chapter*, digital stories can grow beyond these limitations to use locations, characters, or other, more abstract divisions of a story.

For example, an ink story based on a detective speaking to different suspects of a crime might divide itself up into knots based on its characters, as illustrated in the following code snippet:

```
The detective considered the suspects in front of her.

== lady_taylor

== lord_davies

== sir_jones

== lady_turner
```

The name of knots in ink must follow three specific rules, as outlined here:

- They can contain numbers.
- They can contain uppercase and lowercase letters.
- The only special symbol allowed is an underscore.

Spaces cannot be used in the names of knots. Without spaces to break up words, knot names are often written using lowercase letters with an underscore between names, words, or other important details.

Diverting between knots

Creating knots themselves has little usefulness without a way to move between them. In ink, moving between knots is called **diverting**. A *divert* is created by using a minus sign (-) and a greater-than sign (>). This combination, - >, points to which knot the flow will move to next, as illustrated in the following code snippet:

```
-> example_knot
```

```
== example_knot
Some content.
```

Once defined, a knot can be accessed by any other code within the same story. Within an ink story using knots, it is not uncommon for one of the first lines of code to be a divert.

Using DONE and END

The introduction to the concept of a *flow* in *Chapter 1*, *Text, Flow, Choices, and Weaves* mentioned a specific error that all the three previous code examples in this chapter have in common. Because diverting between knots introduces the possibility of creating a complex narrative, ink needs to know at least one ending of the story to stop a story from *running out*. To help signal to ink when a story is going to end, all stories have two built-in knots called DONE and END. Unlike other knots using lowercase and— often— underscores, these are written using uppercase letters.

The differences between DONE and END are in their usage. When a story diverts to DONE (- > DONE), it signals the end of the current flow but not the end of the story. END, however, signals the end of all possible flows and completely ends a story. The use of DONE allows for creating a new flow structure. END stops the story and does not allow for anything else to happen.

Any ink story diverting to a knot, not DONE or END, must divert to either at some point, or the story will be unusable. Returning to the use of `example_knot` earlier in this chapter, a usable form of the code would be this:

Example 1

```
-> example_knot

== example_knot
Some content.
-> DONE
```

Within Inky, the use of the phrase `End of story` displayed at the end of every output is the use of the special knot, END. Without content to show, the story has come to its end. In the terminology of ink, it has diverted to END. Here is a screenshot displaying this:

Some content.

End of story

Figure 2.1 – End of story

Moving between sections

Knots allow authors to divide up an ink story into sections they can name. Diverting allows for moving between these knots. In *Chapter 1, Text, Flow, Choices, and Weaves,* choices were introduced using the asterisk (*) and the ability to branch a story. Using a divert as the result of a choice allows an author to craft a weave, a set of choices, where each could divert to different knots.

For example, returning to the detective example earlier in the chapter, an updated version with choices where each one diverted to knots for the characters would look like this:

Example 2

```
The detective considered the suspects in front of her.


* Lady Taylor
    -> lady_taylor
```

```
* Lord Davies
    -> lord_davies
* Sir Jones
    -> sir_jones
* Lady Turner
    -> lady_turner


== lady_taylor
Standing off to the side of the gathered crowd and looking
out the window was Lady Taylor. She was elegantly dressed in
a cream evening gown and the light from the storm outside was
a stark contrast to the flowing dress and quiet form of the
woman.


The detective made her way over to question her.
-> DONE
== lord_davies
"Ah! Detective!" barked the commanding voice of Lord Davies.
With a drink in his hand and the red evidence of practiced
drinking on his face, he began again. "Over here! I know you
will want to hear what happened from me."


The detective considered the man and then turned to face him.
-> DONE
== sir_jones
The detective turned to the fireplace. Leaning against it was
"Sir Jones." The detective knew this was a nickname for the
person in front of her. They were neither of the rank "sir" in
this area nor was their name "Jones." They had appeared about
six months ago at parties like this one and was quite a fixture
at this point. No one knew much about them other than that they
went by the name "Sir Jones" now.


The detective regarded them for a moment and headed over.
-> DONE
== lady_turner
```

```
Lady Turner had been crying. The evidence of sorrow was etched
into the drying black edges of her makeup at the bottom of her
eyes as she tried to clean up her face. As the detective looked
over, Lady Turner caught her eye and seemed to communicate how
much she did not like to show the evidence of crying on her
face and was trying to clear it quickly.


The detective walked to her and sat down.
-> DONE
```

In the updated version, a *weave* is added. Each choice within it immediately diverts to a knot matching a character. Inside the knots is a use of the built-in DONE knot to let ink know the flow should stop after the content of the knot. In the new code, a much more complex story is created by only using the three concepts of choices, diverts, and knots.

Knots and stitches

Knots allow an ink story to be broken up into different parts. Within a knot, additional subsections can be added, called **stitches**. A *stitch* is created using a single equals sign (=) and its name. Stitches follow the same naming rules of knots: they can contain numbers, letters, and an underscore, but cannot use any other special characters. Stitches can also only appear inside an existing knot.

Returning to the example_knot code, two stitches could be added, as follows:

```
-> example_knot


== example_knot


= stitch_one


= stitch_two
```

The common error of a flow *running out* for knots also applies to stitches. As subsections of a story, they must also either divert to another knot or stitch or use the built-in knots to stop the flow or story. In the following screenshot, you can see an example of a flow running out in a stitch:

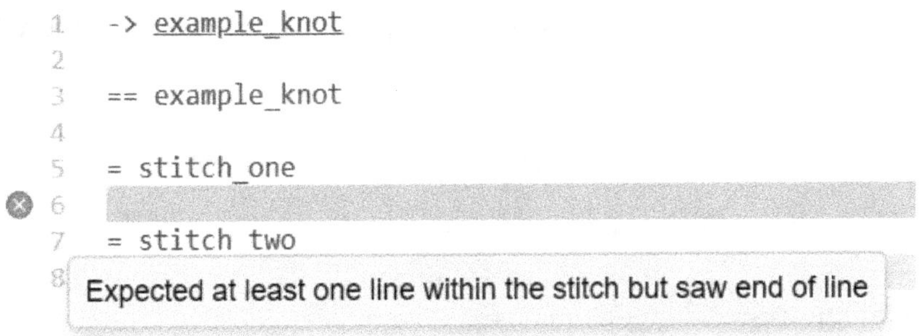

```
1    -> example_knot
2
3    == example_knot
4
5    = stitch_one
6
7    = stitch two
8
```

Expected at least one line within the stitch but saw end of line

Figure 2.2 – An error of flow running out in an example stitch

The first stitch in a knot is an exception to this error. The story will flow from the knot into the first stitch automatically. A corrected version of the previous example, accounting for flowing into the first stitch and including additional diverts, is given here:

Example 3

```
-> example_knot

== example_knot

= stitch_one
Diverting to example_knot will automatically show this.
-> DONE
= stitch_two
-> DONE
```

This would be the output:

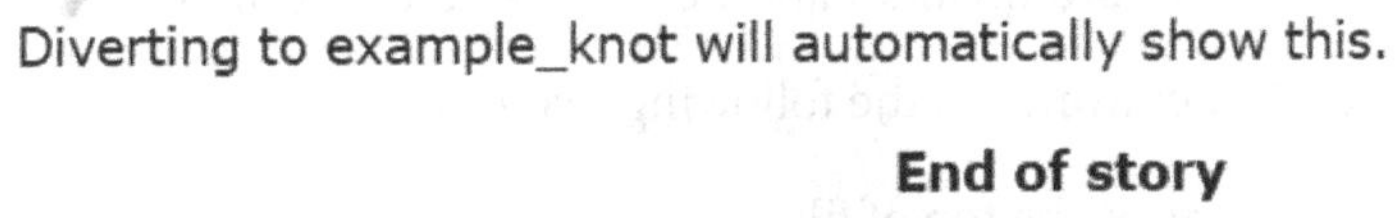

Diverting to example_knot will automatically show this.

End of story

Figure 2.3 – Inky output from diverting to example_knot

As their own subsections of an ink story, stitches can also be accessed directly. Diverting to a stitch inside of a knot follows **dot notation**. A period, dot (.), is used between the name of the divert and the stitch within it.

Diverting directly to `stitch_two` at the top of the previous code would produce the following code:

Example 4

```
-> example_knot.stitch_two

== example_knot

= stitch_one
Diverting to example_knot will automatically show this.
-> DONE
= stitch_two
This will now appear because the stitch is being diverted to
directly.
-> DONE
```

This would be the output:

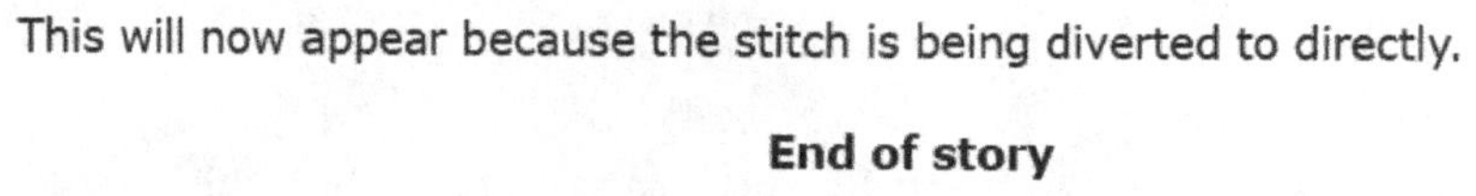

This will now appear because the stitch is being diverted to directly.

End of story

Figure 2.4 – Ink output from diverting to example_knot.stitch_two stitch

Dividing up a story across different files

As new knots and stitches are added to a single file, they can quickly grow very long. To help with this issue, ink has a keyword for combining files: INCLUDE. When used with ink code, the INCLUDE keyword includes another file based on its filename.

The use of the INCLUDE keyword has the following two rules:

- It should only be used at the top of files.
- It cannot be used inside knots.

In Inky, additional files can be added to an existing project by using the **New Included ink File** menu option, as illustrated in the following screenshot, and naming the new file:

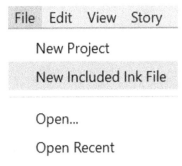

Figure 2.5 – Inky's New Included Ink File menu option

Using this functionality with the main ink file option also adds a single newline to the existing ink file, if it exists. For example, creating an additionalFile.ink file will generate an additional line of code: INCLUDE additionalFile.ink.

> **Warning**
>
> Inky does not automatically add .ink to a filename when creating included ink files. It is strongly recommended to always add the file type when using this functionality.

Every use of INCLUDE adds the file to the current project. This means any knots and stitches in these included files can be accessed by any others. Because files can be named after locations, characters, or other abstractions in the story, this allows an author to break a story into different files with their own knots and stitches, as shown in the following code example:

Example 5

```
INCLUDE books.ink
You stand in front of a shelf with two books.


* [Red Book]
    -> books.red_book
* [Blue Book]
    -> books.blue_book
```

Each choice diverts to a stitch in another file in the new example. Because Inky uses INCLUDE to combine files into a single project, the knots and stitches as part of the books.ink file can be accessed as if all the code were part of one file, as illustrated in the following code example:

Example 5 (books.ink)

```
== books

= red_book
The red book slides open as a deep, masculine voice fills your
mind.
-> DONE
= blue_book
The blue book slowly flips open as a reluctant, feminine voice
creeps into your thoughts.
-> DONE
```

Flow runs top to bottom in ink. Starting with the first file, the flow would show the weave of two choices. Choosing the Red Book option would then divert to the stitch in the other file and, ultimately, to the use of the divert in the DONE special knot, as illustrated in the following screenshot:

You stand in front of a shelf with two books.

The red book slides open as a deep masculine voice fills your mind.

End of story

Figure 2.6 – Combined output from Red Book choice in Example 5

Looping knots

A knot can divert to itself. This fundamental concept is an important part of the advanced dialog and narrative structures in ink. However, care must be taken when having knots divert to themselves or in a looping pattern. It can become very easy to create **infinite loops** where the code loops without stopping. To prevent this error, it is always a good idea to include a weave with at least one choice whose content ends the story or breaks the loop.

By combining choices, diverts, and knots, looping structures can be created. Within these structures, sticky choices become important for creating consistent options for readers to choose from during each loop.

Looping structures

The most basic looping structure has two choices. The first continues the loop and the second must end the story somehow, as illustrated in the following code example:

Example 6

```
You look at the rock in front of you.
-> rock


== rock
* Push the rock up the hill.
    -> rock
* Ignore the rock for now.
    -> DONE
```

Choices, those created with an asterisk (*), can only be used once in an entire story. In the previous example, if the first option is chosen, the loop repeats, but the second option then appears as the only one, as illustrated in the following screenshot:

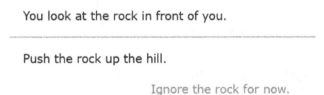

Figure 2.7 – Example 6 choices after one loop

In some stories, reducing the options as the reader moves through the story could work well, but a different type of choice is needed for those cases where the same options are needed for every loop: **sticky choices**.

Revisiting sticky choices

In *Chapter 1, Text, Flow, Choices, and Weaves*, sticky choices were introduced. Shown as part of a flow moving from top to bottom and without repeating any sections, sticky choices did not seem very useful at the time. However, within looping patterns using diverts and knots, sticky choices are often the best type of choice to use, as illustrated in the following code example:

Example 7

```
You look at the rock in front of you.
-> rock


== rock
+ Push the rock up the hill.
    -> rock
+ Ignore the rock for now.
    -> rock
```

In the updated code, both options are sticky choices. This new code allows for a repeating pattern and consistent weave options regardless of loop count, as illustrated in the following screenshot:

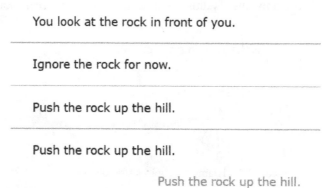

You look at the rock in front of you.

Ignore the rock for now.

Push the rock up the hill.

Push the rock up the hill.

Push the rock up the hill.

Figure 2.8 – Inky output from multiple loops of Example 7

Detecting and changing options

Knots and stitches are not the only ink concept capable of looping—options can do so as well. They also have the unique ability to detect when they are part of looping structures. These special types of options are named **labeled options**. They create an ability to give a *label* to an option and track if it has been seen before in the story. Labels are also an example of a **variable**: a value changed as part of the story by code.

The use of labeled options enables us to use the second type of option: **conditional options**. As with their labeled sisters, conditional options are part of the option, but they do not track loops. Instead, they *conditionally* show the option. If the comparison is true, the option is shown. If it is not, the option is hidden.

Labeled and conditional options

Labeled options are created using open and closing parentheses around a name after the symbol for a choice, a plus sign (+) or asterisk (*), and the text of the choice itself. Labeled options follow the same rules as the name of knots and stitches: they can contain numbers, uppercase and lowercase letters, and an underscore. They cannot contain spaces or other special symbols. This is illustrated in the following code snippet:

```
You look at the rock in front of you.
-> rock


== rock
+ (push) Push the rock up the hill.
    -> rock
* Push the rock over the edge.
    -> DONE
```

In the new example code, a label called push is added to the first option and exists as a variable in the story. Because it is part of the option itself, its value will be increased every time the option is revisited in the story. This allows an author to test whether the player has been picking the same option multiple times. The following code example illustrates this:

Example 8

```
You look at the rock in front of you.
-> rock
```

```
== rock
+ (push) Push the rock up the hill.
    -> rock
* {push >= 4} Push the rock over the edge.
    -> DONE
```

In the latest change, a conditional option has also been added using open—{—and closing—}—curly brackets around the comparison between a variable and a value. In the new code, when the story starts, the reader can choose the Push the rock up the hill option. As they do, the value of the label for the option also increases. Once its value is at least 4, the second option becomes available, and the reader can push the rock over the edge, as illustrated in the following screenshot:

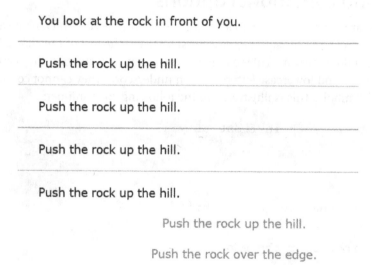

You look at the rock in front of you.

Push the rock up the hill.

Push the rock up the hill.

Push the rock up the hill.

Push the rock up the hill.

Push the rock up the hill.

Push the rock over the edge.

Figure 2.9 – Push the rock up the hill chosen four times in Example 8

Conditional and labeled options can also be combined. However, the order in which they appear is important. Labels must appear in front of conditional options. They cannot appear in the other order, as illustrated in the following code example:

Example 9

```
You look at the rock in front of you.
-> rock


== rock
```

```
+ (push) {push < 6} Push the rock up the hill.
    -> rock
* {push >= 6} Push the rock over the edge.
    -> DONE
```

In the new example code, the reader only sees a single option when the story starts. They must make the same choice six times before the first option is removed and the second becomes available. Once the reader selects this option, the story finally ends.

Building dynamic weaves

Sticky choices enable options to remain across loops created by diverting to the same knot. Labeled and conditional options allow for tracking and showing certain options after certain conditions are met in a story. Using all these concepts, dynamic weaves become possible, as illustrated in the following code example:

Example 10

```
You pause to double-check check the folder again. Yes, you have
all the evidence here.

You nod at your partner and he enters the other room. You take
a breath and open the door.

The suspect sits in front of you. As you take a seat, she turns
to look at you.

-> interrogation


== interrogation
+ (knife) {knife < 1} [Ask about the knife]
    The suspect shakes their head. "I don't know nothing!"
    -> interrogation
+ (knife_again) {knife == 1 && knife_again < 1} [Ask about the
    knife again.]
    You take a picture of the knife out of the folder and put
        it down on the table without saying another word.
    -> interrogation
+ (knife_once_again) {knife_again == 1 && knife_once_again < 1}
```

```
[Ask about the knife one more time.]
    "Yes. Fine. It's mine," the suspect replies and crosses
       her arms. Looking at them, you notice the slight cuts on
       the underside of her arm.
    -> interrogation
+ (cuts) {knife_once_again == 1 && cuts < 1} [Ask about the
  cuts on her arm.]
    You point to the cuts on her arms.
    She shrugs. "It was an accident."
    You frown and point at the knife.
    "It's my knife, yes," she says, looking away.
    -> interrogation
+ {cuts == 1} [Take out the picture of the gun next.]
    "This is not yours, though," you say, taking out the
       picture.
    She does not look back.
    "He attacked you. And not for the first time," you say
       and point to the older scars still visible. "You finally
       had enough. You shot him."
    She still looks away, but you can see her shoulders slump.
       She knows that you know.
    -> DONE
```

In the new code, complex combinations of labels and conditional options are used to track information during the interrogation of the suspect. Making one choice unlocks the next in order, as the flow loops back to the same knot as information is slowly unlocked and the reader learns more through making one choice at a time.

> **Note**
>
> Some conditional options in *Example 10* use two ampersands, &&. This is known as **logical AND**. It tests the first condition and, if it is true, it checks the next. If both are true, the entire combination is true.

In the next chapter, easier ways to create sequences of information will be covered, as well as introducing randomness into creating text and options. Instead of using diverts and knots, ink supplies much simpler functionality for doing the same general actions and building repetitions explicitly using knots each time.

Summary

This chapter introduced you to knots, sections of a story, and diverts, which are ways to move between them. We examined the use of DONE and END as built-in knots to end a flow (DONE) and stop a story completely (END). Stitches, subsections of a knot, were then discussed to break up a story into even more parts. We learned that the INCLUDE keyword can be used to break a story into separate files and be *included* as part of the same project.

Knots can divert to themselves. This, as we saw, is the key to creating looping structures where the use of other concepts, labeled and conditional options, can also be combined. Labels allow us to create variables for tracking how many times an option has been shown. Labeled options then led on to using conditional options, testing how many times an option has been chosen when using a looping structure. Finally, we ended with making a dynamic weave, using a looping structure where each choice made changed the values of labels and unlocked each choice in order.

In the next chapter, we will build on the concepts of knots and diverts. By navigating to different sections of a story, alternatives, an ink concept where different text is shown across a story or because of multiple loops, becomes possible. This allows ink to react to readers revisiting knots and options to show different content.

Questions

1. What is a knot?
2. What is the difference between DONE and END?
3. What is a stitch?
4. How can INCLUDE be used in ink?
5. What is the difference between a labeled and a conditional option?

3
Sequences, Cycles, and Shuffling Text

This chapter introduces the concept of **alternatives**, programmable ways of introducing additional text, and advanced code that can react to loops. We will cover each type of alternative (**sequence, cycle**, and **shuffle**) in turn and look at how they can be combined with looping structures in ink. Next, we will examine **multi-line alternatives**, functionality for defining more complex structures based on the type of alternative used to create them. Finally, we will close the chapter with **nested alternatives**, the use of one or more alternatives inside each other.

In this chapter, we will to cover the following main topics:

- Using alternatives
- Creating multi-line alternatives
- Nesting alternatives

Technical requirements

The examples used in this chapter, in `*.ink` files, can be found online on GitHub:
`https://github.com/PacktPublishing/Dynamic-Story-Scripting-with-the-ink-Scripting-Language/tree/main/Chapter3`.

Using alternatives

In *Chapter 2, Knots, Diverts, and Looping Patterns*, the use of opening, {, and closing, }, curly brackets signaled the use of a conditional option. Between using labels and conditions, options could become dynamic and react to the reader making choices between loops. However, curly brackets are used for more than conditional options. In ink, they also signal the use of any *code*, and one of the most common forms of code is the use of an **alternative**. Used to create different text effects and react to loops, alternatives separate each of their elements by a vertical bar, |. Depending on the type of alternative used, different text effects can happen.

Sequences

The first and default alternative is a **sequence**. As its name might suggest, a sequence is a series of values. They are accessed based on their name, *in sequence*:

Example 1:

```
It was a {dark and stormy night|bright and shining day}.
```

In *Example 1*, a sequence is used. It has two elements, `dark and stormy night` and `bright and shining day`, with a vertical bar between them. When first run, the sequence would produce the following output:

```
It was a dark and stormy night.
```

In a sequence, any elements beyond the first are only shown when the sequence is run additional times. In other words, a sequence with more than one element works best inside a looping structure:

Example 2:

```
She looked out the window.
-> weather
== weather
+ What was the weather like?
    It was a {dark and stormy night|bright and shining day}.
    -> weather
* Ignore the weather.
    -> DONE
```

By diverting back to the knot, `weather`, a loop is created. This allows the second element of the sequence to be shown on the second loop:

Figure 3.1 – Screenshot of Inky showing both elements from Example 2

A sequence only continues if new elements are within it. Once a sequence reaches its end, it stops on the last element. In *Example 2*, choosing the option **What was the weather like?** would not move to the first element. With only two elements, the last one, `bright and shining day`, would be shown again:

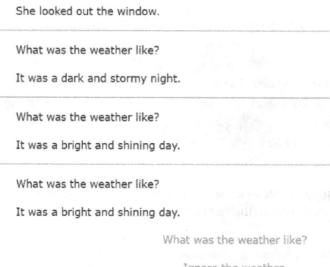

She looked out the window.

What was the weather like?
It was a dark and stormy night.

What was the weather like?
It was a bright and shining day.

What was the weather like?
It was a bright and shining day.

What was the weather like?
Ignore the weather.

Figure 3.2 – Screenshot of Inky showing the repeating element from Example 2

Important note

Example 2 follows a pattern established in *Chapter 2, Knots, Diverts, and Looping Patterns*, with two choices. The first loops the structure and the second breaks it. Always use choices when creating loops to avoid creating ones that cannot end!

Sequences are best used in situations where a user might exhaust a series of elements and end on the last one. When a repeating sequence is needed, a different concept is used: **cycles**.

Cycles

Like sequences, **cycles** are also created using open and closing curly brackets. However, cycles include an ampersand, &, in front of the first element in the set. This tells ink to *cycle* the elements and return to the first after the last:

Example 3:

```
He flipped the calendar, looking at each month in turn.
-> calendar
== calendar
+ [Flip pages]
    He saw the month was {&January|February|March|April|May|
        June|July|August|September|October|November|December}.
    -> calendar
* Put down calendar.
    -> DONE
```

In *Example 3*, the looping structure reruns the cycle, moving through all the months and then *cycling* back to the first element again:

Figure 3.3 – Screenshot of ink showing all elements from the Example 3 cycle

All alternatives can contain empty elements. For cycles, any blank elements count towards the total number. It is possible to create a cycle that shows elements only after a certain number of loops:

Example 4:

```
He awoke to the sudden darkness. He tried to bend his elbows
outward and his arms stopped against some sort of wall.
Carefully bringing his arms up, he pressed his palms out and
hit another surface inches from his face.
```
```
Desperate to figure out where he was, he remembered he still
had his lighter in his pocket. Shifting the left side of his
body against the wall, he reached the tips of his right hand
into his back pocket and drew it out.
```
```
-> lighter
```
```
== lighter
```
```
+ [Try lighter]
```
```
    {&|||For a moment, there was light before the flame went
out.}
```
```
    -> lighter
```

Using empty elements with a cycle can be very effective for creating a situation where the reader must take an action multiple times before a result happens. In *Example 4*, the cycle has multiple empty elements separated by vertical bars. The last element, `For a moment, there was light before the flame went out.`, is only shown after the reader chooses the option **Try lighter** four times:

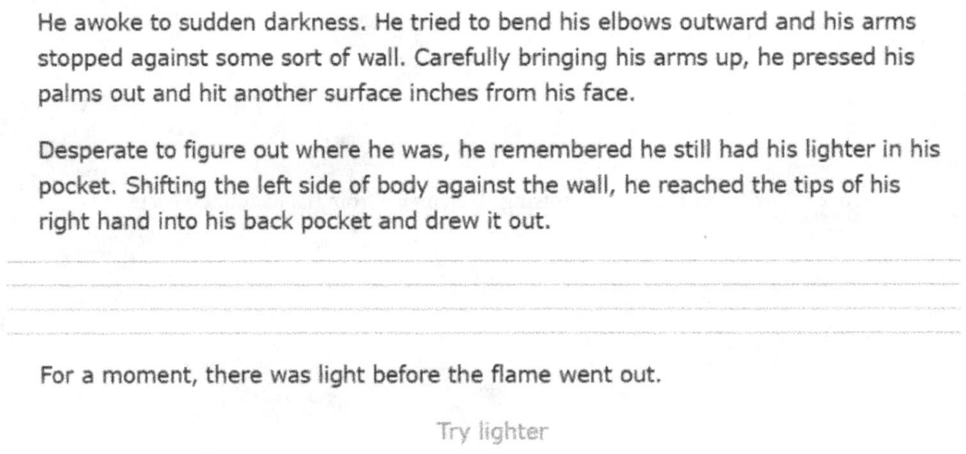

He awoke to sudden darkness. He tried to bend his elbows outward and his arms stopped against some sort of wall. Carefully bringing his arms up, he pressed his palms out and hit another surface inches from his face.

Desperate to figure out where he was, he remembered he still had his lighter in his pocket. Shifting the left side of body against the wall, he reached the tips of his right hand into his back pocket and drew it out.

For a moment, there was light before the flame went out.

Try lighter

Figure 3.4 – Screenshot of Inky showing Example 4's use of empty elements

Shuffles

Shuffles are a type of alternative where elements are accessed at random. Like cycles, shuffles also use a special symbol. A shuffle is created when a tilde, ~, appears before the first element in the set:

Example 5:

```
The lucky number for today is {~1|2|3|4|5|6|7|8|9|10}.
```

Unlike sequences and cycles, shuffles do not show their elements in order. Combined with empty elements, as shown previously with cycles, the chances of an element being picked are always consistent with the total number of elements. This means that to create a shuffle where one of its elements is shown 1 of 10 runs, the code would be the following:

Example 6:

```
One out of ten runs of this shuffle will produce the number 10:
{~|||||||||10}
```

In *Example 6*, element 10 has a 10% chance of appearing. Most runs (90%) would not see it, creating a unique moment for those users encountering the event within their narrative experience of the story's content:

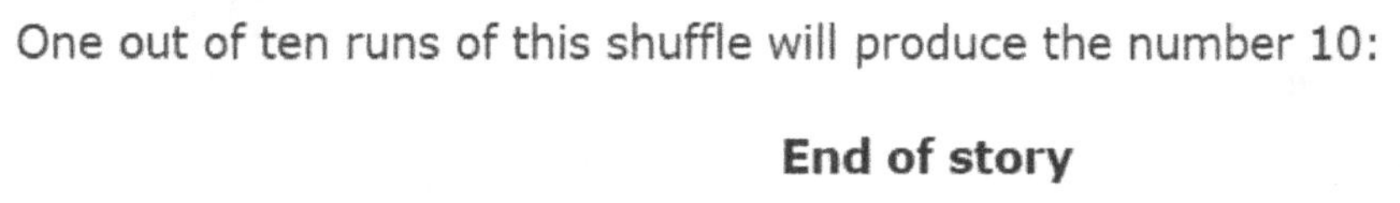

One out of ten runs of this shuffle will produce the number 10:

End of story

Figure 3.5 – Screenshot of Inky showing the output of Example 6 without element 10

Creating multi-line alternatives

Sequences, cycles, and shuffles can be written using one single line of code. However, all alternatives can also be written using their multi-line form. For each of these, curly brackets are still used, but each element is on its own line with a dash, -, appearing before it.

Multi-line cycles

To create a multi-line cycle, the keyword `cycle` is used with a colon, `:`, and with each element on its own line:

Example 7:

```
He flipped the calendar, looking at each month in turn.
-> calendar
== calendar
+ [Flip pages]
    He saw the month was <>{cycle:
    - January
    - February
    - March
    - April
    - May
    - June
    - July
    - August
    - September
    - October
    - November
    - December
    }<>.
    -> calendar
* Put down calendar.
    -> DONE
```

Any use of multi-line alternatives also introduces a new issue. Because each element is on its own line, each is also considered a *line* by ink. This means its output would introduce additional spacing between lines. To help with this issue, **glue** can be used between the multi-line alternative and the next text content.

> **Reminder**
>
> *Chapter 1, Text, Flow, Choices, and Weaves*, introduced the concept of **glue**, the use of the less-than and greater-than symbols together. This concept *glues* one line to the end of the previous. With multi-line alternatives, the use of glue removes the additional space between its output and the next line of content.

Multi-line sequences

Multi-line cycles use the keyword `cycle` and multi-line shuffles use the keyword `shuffle`. However, multi-line sequences use the keyword `stopping`:

Example 8:

```
She looked out the window.
-> weather
== weather
+ What was the weather like?
    It was a <>{stopping:
    - dark and stormy night
    - bright and shining day
    }<>.
    -> weather
* Ignore the weather.
    -> DONE
```

Multi-line sequences also introduce an important difference between themselves and their one-line forms: readability. Each element in a multi-line alternative is separated by a new line. In the one-line form, a sequence with a particularly long text element would be hard to differentiate between its end and the start of the next element in the alternative:

```
{This is one really long line that keeps going and going just
to make sure that it wraps to a new line.|This is more content
as part of this second element.}
```

Broken into new lines, the previous code can become much easier to edit and understand:

Example 9:

```
{stopping:
- This is one really long line that keeps going and going to
make sure that it wraps to a new line.
- This is more content as part of this second element.
}
```

Nesting alternatives

Sequences, cycles, and shuffles can all be nested *inside* each other. When this happens, the combined form is what is known as a **nested alternative**, where one alternative appears as the element of another.

Combining cycles and shuffles

Within a looping structure, a cycle can be very useful to repeat content after a certain number of loops. When combined with a shuffle, random content can be selected from the shuffle and then repeated within the larger cycle. For example, to generate a new random number for each loop, a cycle with a single element using multiple shuffles would produce this effect using only one line of code:

Example 10:

```
Her hands were sweating, and her head hurt. She just needed to
enter the correct digits into the controls and the vault would
open. Once she got in and away with the treasure inside, she
could be done with this job and leave this life behind. She had
sworn there would only be one more job like this one job ago.
This was truly the last one, she decided again.
```

```
She wiped her forehead and considered the controls again.
```

```
-> combination
```

```
== combination
```

```
What was the combination again?
```

```
+ [Was it {&{~1|2|3|4|5}-{~1|2|3|4|5}-{~1|2|3|4|5}}?]
```

```
    -> combination
```

```
* Give up on the controls. This was hopeless. She could not
remember the numbers.
```

```
    -> DONE
```

Example 10 uses a cycle and three shuffles. Each time the loop runs, the cycle reruns. With only one element, it *cycles* again and reruns the shuffles, each of which picks a random number from one to five. This has the effect of generating a new three-digit number for each loop:

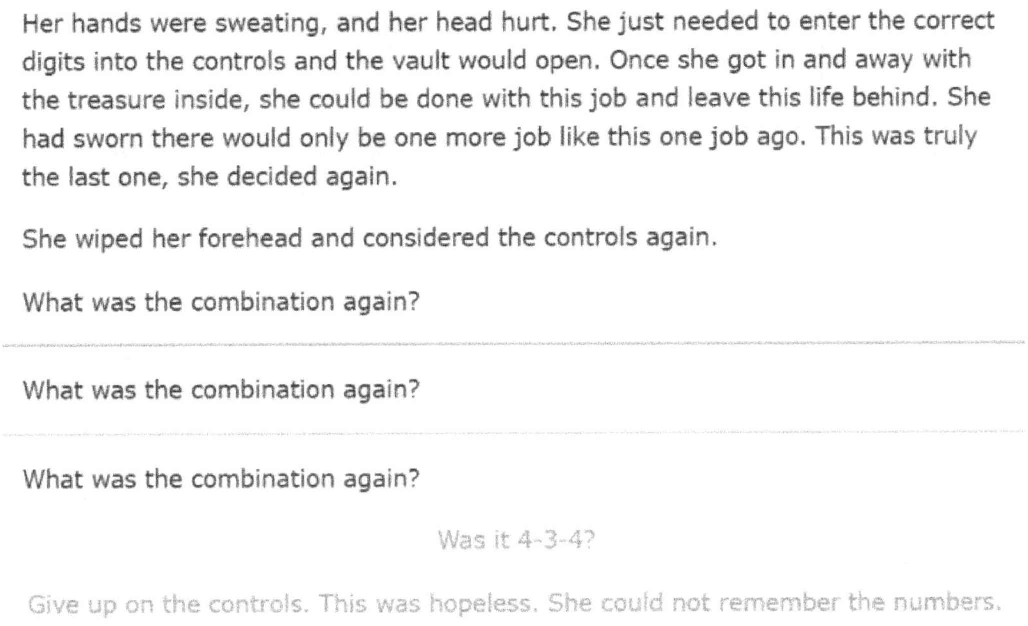

Her hands were sweating, and her head hurt. She just needed to enter the correct digits into the controls and the vault would open. Once she got in and away with the treasure inside, she could be done with this job and leave this life behind. She had sworn there would only be one more job like this one job ago. This was truly the last one, she decided again.

She wiped her forehead and considered the controls again.

What was the combination again?

What was the combination again?

What was the combination again?

Was it 4-3-4?

Give up on the controls. This was hopeless. She could not remember the numbers.

Figure 3.6 – Screenshot of Inky showing random three-digit numbers across loops from Example 10

The code in *Example 10* also demonstrates something not previously made explicit about how alternatives work in ink. The elements of alternatives often have text content, and options are created from the text of choices. This means that alternatives can be used with choices to generate dynamic options. This also means that diverts can be elements of alternatives as well.

For example, a set of diverts can be used with a shuffle to move the reader to different points at random based on the options they chose:

Example 11:

```
They stood before the doorway at the end of the hallway.
Without knowing where it would go, they reached out.
* [Open door]
    {~-> treasure|-> back_in_hallway}
== treasure
Yes! The room was full of treasure.
-> DONE
== back_in_hallway
As the door opened, there was a flash, and they blinked several
```

```
times before realizing what had happened. They were back in
front of the door. No!
-> DONE
```

When run, the combination of diverts and a shuffle in *Example 11* would randomly pick between two possible branches. The reader would either be diverted to the `treasure` or `back_in_hallway` knots.

Shuffling shuffles

In both *Example 10* and *Example 11*, one type of alternative was combined with another. It is also possible to nest the same type of alternative. Shuffles can be nested within other shuffles to make advanced combinatorial results. For example, it is possible to generate a quick history of a fantasy kingdom by defining possible years and events, and then using one-line shuffles inside a multi-line shuffle to build a sentence describing the kingdom:

Example 12:

```
It was the
<> {shuffle:
- year {~1|2|3|4|5|6|7|8|9}{~1|2|3|4|5|6|7|8|9} of the New
    Era
- {~second|third|fourth|fifth|sixth|seventh} {~Year of the
    Frog|Year of the Snake}
    }
<> and our kingdom
<> {shuffle:
- {~was doing well|was facing a crisis}
- {~was at war|was recovering from a war} with {~the
    giants|the elves|the humans}
    }
<>.
```

In *Example 12*, the use of the single-line shuffles creates all of the small details of the kingdom. These are then used within the larger multi-line shuffles for the major events. They build a history based on different elements *shuffled* together:

It was the fifth Year of the Frog and our kingdom was recovering from a war with the humans.

End of story

Figure 3.7 – Screenshot of Inky showing of one of the many possible outputs of Example 12

Alternatives and their multi-line forms can be very useful for detecting and acting on loops by using sequences and cycles to show new or change old content. Shuffles, with the ability to introduce randomness in a story, are an easy way to generate dynamic text in a story, as shown in *Example 12*.

When combining different types of alternatives, such as those used in *Example 10*, these *nested* alternatives can generate complex content based on how each type works individually. However, what was not covered and is introduced in the next chapter is a way to save what is generated by an alternative and then compare values. As with the story used in *Example 10*, generating a random three-digit number is useful, but saving and remembering it is even better. *Chapter 4, Variables, Lists, and Functions*, introduces how to retain values across a story as generated by alternatives and changed because of a user's interactions in ink.

Summary

In this chapter, we looked at the seemingly simple concept of alternatives. In ink, the three types of alternatives are sequences, cycles, and shuffles. Each provides a different way of accessing its elements. Sequences show each element in turn until its last one. Cycles repeat their elements, looping back to the first element after encountering the end. Shuffles select a random element from their set each time they are run, creating a way to introduce randomness to stories for the first time.

Alternatives can also be expressed in both one-line and multi-line forms. When written in their longer multi-line forms, alternatives use a keyword for their type and have each element on a separate line. While much easier to read for an author, we reviewed how care must be taken to incorporate glue because of how ink interprets each line of text in a story.

Finally, we learned alternatives can be combined in a nested form. An element of an alternative can be another alternative. When used together, this showed how, for example, a cycle and shuffle can be combined to regenerate random selections from multiple shuffles each time they are run. We also saw how the text of elements from alternatives can be used with choices and even how diverts can be elements of alternatives.

In the next chapter, we will see how to create and access the values of variables in ink.

Q&A

1. What are the three types of alternatives in ink?
2. What special symbol is used between elements in their single-line form?
3. What special symbol is used before the first element in the set to create a cycle?
4. What is the difference between a sequence and a cycle?
5. What is unique about a shuffle?
6. What is the keyword used to create a multi-line sequence?

4
Variables, Lists, and Functions

This chapter builds on multiple concepts that were introduced in *Chapter 2, Knots, Diverts, and Looping Patterns*. In the first topic, we will examine how the keyword VAR works with a single value in ink, and how it can be combined with **alternatives**. Once values have been saved, they can be changed as part of larger looping structures. In the second topic, we will work with multiple variables together using the LIST keyword.

In ink, we can group variables into a concept called a list. We will also examine how to create and change the values that are part of a list. We will then review when they are best used in a project and situations where multiple, single variables might work better. This discussion will move us on to the next topic, where we will look at working with functions.

Values that are part of a list can be changed by other concepts called **functions**. In the third topic, we will *call* some of the built-in functions to work with different list values. These will allow us to perform actions across a list, such as determining the number of entries or picking one out at random. Working with functions will help us prepare for the next step, which is creating functions.

In the last topic, we will explore how to create our functions in ink. As we will see, functions allow us to define small tasks or series of actions we can use multiple times by calling the created function. Functions, as we will learn, are special forms of **knots** in ink. This means we can send data to a function as well as a knot. However, only functions can return data.

In this chapter, we will cover the following main topics:

- Storing values using VAR
- Working with LIST
- Calling functions
- Making new functions and calling knots

Technical requirements

The examples used in this chapter, in `*.ink` files, can be found online on GitHub: `https://github.com/PacktPublishing/Dynamic-Story-Scripting-with-the-ink-Scripting-Language/tree/main/Chapter4`.

Storing values using VAR

In *Chapter 2, Knots, Diverts, and Looping Patterns*, variables were introduced as a part of using labeled options within the weaves of looping structures in ink. By creating a label, an option could record whether it had been shown before. This allowed us to keep track of the number of loops within a knot easily. Within ink, labeled options are one form of a more general concept for storing and changing any kind of value. This more general form uses a special keyword: **VAR**.

The VAR keyword creates a variable that's capable of storing different types of data. Variables created with the VAR keyword can store numbers (including decimal values), **strings** (collections of letters, numbers, and special symbols enclosed in single-quotation or double-quotation marks), **Booleans** (`true` or `false` values), and even diverts. Variables created using the VAR keyword are also *global*: they can be accessed by any code that is part of the overall project.

Variable names that use the VAR keyword in ink follow the same rules as that of knots and stitches:

- They can contain numbers.
- They can contain uppercase and lowercase letters.
- The only special symbol that's allowed is an underscore.

Like the naming conventions for knots and stitches, an underscore is often used between words within the name of the variable:

Example 1 (Example1.ink):

```
VAR reader_name = "Dan"
```

Variables are given values by an operation called **assignment**. You can use the equals sign (=) to assign the variable the value following the sign on the same line. It is common to include a single space between the name of the variable, the equals sign (=), and the value being assigned to the variable.

There is one explicit rule that must always be followed when using the VAR keyword and assigning a variable its initial value: whatever the value is, it must be static. In ink, this means that the first assignment of any variable cannot be a combination of other, existing values or the result of code performing mathematical operations.

Once created, however, the value of the variable can be changed, but the initial assignment must always exist first and not be the result of any computation.

In this topic, we will learn how to show and change variable values. Because alternatives (covered in *Chapter 3, Sequences, Cycles, and Shuffling Text*) produce values, we will also explore how to save what they produce and use that value as part of additional code.

Showing variables

The use of opening, {, and closing, }, curly brackets in ink signals the use of code. When combined with the name of a variable, ink will substitute the value of the variable as part of the surrounding text. This allows an author to use variables as part of the text and have ink switch the name of the variable with its value in its final output:

Example 2 (Example2.ink):

```
VAR reader_name = "Dan"
```

```
The name of the reader is {reader_name}.
```

When the code in *Example 2* is run, ink creates a variable named `reader_name`. Next, it sets the variable to the value of `"Dan"`. When it encounters the text, ink understands that the curly brackets are code and switches the name of the variable for its value:

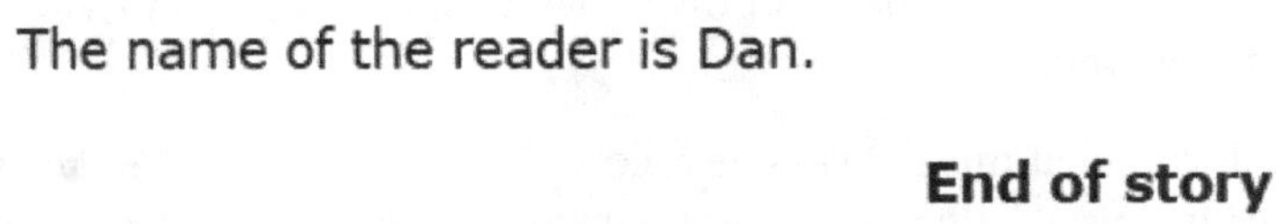

The name of the reader is Dan.

End of story

Figure 4.1 – Screenshot of ink's output for Example 2

The use of curly brackets signals the use of *any* code in ink. This means that mathematical operations can also be performed inside curly brackets on variables. ink will substitute the resulting value as part of the final output, as shown in the following example:

Example 3 (Example3.ink):

```
VAR first_variable = 2
VAR second_variable = 2
```

```
Adding the values of the two variables together produces:
   {first_variable + second_variable}.
```

In *Example 3*, there are two variables. Each holds a separate, numerical value. When ink encounters the use of curly brackets, it substitutes the value of each variable with its name. Next, because the curly brackets also contain the addition symbol, ink adds the two numbers together:

Adding the values of the two variables together produces: 4.

End of story

Figure 4.2 – Screenshot of ink's output for Example 3

Depending on the types of data involved, mathematical operations may not always produce the expected output based on experiences with other programming and scripting languages. For example, operations such as addition (using the plus symbol, +), subtraction (using the hyphen, -), multiplication (using the asterisk, *), and division (using the forward slash, /) will all work on numerical values:

Example 4 (Example4.ink):

```
VAR number_two = 2

2 * 2 = {number_two * 2}
2 + 3 = {number_two + 3}
6 / 2 = {6 / number_two}
9 - 2 = {9 - number_two}
```

Using mathematical operations with numerical and string values will produce errors. The only valid way to use mathematic symbols with string values is to use the plus symbol (+). This performs the **concatenation** operation: when a numerical or string value is *added* to an existing string value, it produces a new string value, as shown in the following example:

Example 5 (Example5.ink):

```
VAR example_string = "Hi"

Perform concatenation: {example_string + 3}
```

When the code in *Example 5* is run, ink creates a variable with a string value. However, when it encounters text and curly brackets, it does not perform mathematics. Instead, it *concatenates* the value of the example_string variable with the number 3. This produces a combination of both values in its output:

Perform concatenation: Hi3

End of story

Figure 4.3 – Screenshot of ink's output for Example 5

Let's now move to the next part and understand how to update variables.

Updating variables

Variables can change values. Once a variable is created in ink using the VAR keyword, it can be accessed and its value can be changed at any point within the same code. However, while ink understands that the initial assignment of a variable must be separate from text, we must use a special symbol when changing the value of a variable: a tilde (~). For example, we can create a variable using the VAR keyword and then change its value later in the same code:

Example 6 (Example6.ink):

```
VAR reader_name = "Dan"


The reader's name is {reader_name}.


~ reader_name = "Jesse"


The reader's name is now {reader_name}.
```

If a line of code starts with a tilde (~), this lets ink know that some type of code will occur on this single line. For example, when an initial value is assigned to the variable, ink understands something code-related will be following the tilde (~).

We can create variables using the VAR keyword and update them with code lines starting with a tilde (~). However, as we saw in *Chapter 3, Sequences, Cycles, and Shuffling Text,* **alternatives** allow us to generate a value from a set. As we will see in the next section, we can save the generated value in variables and use it in later parts of the same code.

Storing the current values of alternatives

Alternatives were introduced in *Chapter 3, Sequences, Cycles, and Shuffling Text.* They are used to generate *alternative* text content based on the number of times they had been accessed during looping structures. Because alternatives generate text, their output can also be saved in variables:

Example 7 (Example7.ink):

```
VAR day_of_week = ""
~ day_of_week = "{~Monday|Tuesday|Wednesday|Thursday
```

```
    |Friday|Saturday|Sunday}"
-> calendar

== calendar
Today is {day_of_week}!
-> DONE
```

Instead of needing to rerun an alternative to generate new text, a **shuffle** can have its output saved for future use. This allows the value to be incorporated into other code without the need to recreate the alternative.

Alternatives generate content when they're run. This means that they cannot be used as part of the initial assignment of a variable in ink. The reason for this is that ink handles the creation of variables *before* it runs any alternatives. The generated values of any alternative do not exist when variables are created initially. Because of this, a common pattern is to create a variable with an initial value and then overwrite this value with the generated output of an alternative later in the code.

In *Example 7*, quotation marks enclose the use of a shuffle alternative to create a string value. When run, the shuffle will generate a value that will then become a string, based on the quotation marks around it. As a string value, it will then be able to be used with the assignment line with the tilde (~).

Saving the output of an alternative in ink always requires at least two lines of code. The first is used to create a variable using the VAR keyword with its initial value, while the second is reassigned its value to what is generated by the alternative when the code is run. As was explained in the introduction to the *Storing values using VAR* topic, the explicit rule for using the VAR keyword is that the initial value must exist when the variable is created. The output that's produced by an alternative is considered dynamic, and the initial value of a variable using the VAR keyword must be static.

In this topic, we worked with single values. We started by creating new variables using the VAR keyword and then learned how to update their values with lines beginning with tildes (~). We also explored how the output from an alternative can be saved, but that the variable must be set to an initial value and then updated to the dynamic output produced by the alternative. In the next topic, we will build on the use of variables and create a collection of them using a new keyword called LIST.

Working with LIST

Each use of the VAR keyword creates a single value. In many projects, a handful of single values would be enough to track anything needed while running. However, there are contexts where a set of values might be needed. For these cases, ink has a special keyword called **LIST** that creates a *list* of possible values.

The values of a list can be thought of as possible *states* of its variable. For example, for a LIST named days_of_week, possible values might be the 7 days of the week. These could be defined with LIST itself and then assigned as needed instead of the need to use string values for each day of the week.

In ink, a list defines a new collection of values within the context of the project. Once created, the values of a list can act as possible values for other variables using the VAR keyword.

However, while powerful in its ability to create new possible values for variables, the values that are created have some limitations and often need extra functionality to perform some common operations that are available to other types of data in ink. (LIST functions will be covered in the *Using LIST functions* section, later in this chapter.)

In this topic, we will begin by creating a list of values. We will explore how to use the LIST keyword to create this collection. Then, we will change the values that are part of the collection by following the same pattern that we learned about for working with single values.

Making a LIST

A new list can be created by using the LIST keyword. On a line starting with the LIST keyword, the name of the list is followed by the equals sign (=), and its values are separated by commas. The name of a list, as with other variables in ink, must only contain numbers, letters, and an underscore character. It cannot contain other special symbols or spaces.

Unlike the use of the VAR keyword, when values are assigned to a list, spaces are ignored, including additional, empty lines between one value and the next. Variables that are created by the VAR keyword must be defined on a single line. The values of a list can be spread across multiple lines:

Example 8 (Example8.ink):

```
LIST days_of_week =
Monday,
```

```
Tuesday,

Wednesday,

Thursday,

Friday,

Saturday,

Sunday


VAR day = Monday


Today is {day}.
```

In *Example 8*, a list was created with seven possible values. Next, one of its values, Monday, was assigned to the variable that was created with the VAR keyword. Finally, the last line of code shows the value of day:

Today is Monday.

End of story

Figure 4.4 – Screenshot of ink's output for Example 8

Like with a variable created with the VAR keyword, the values of a list, once created, can also be updated. This follows the pattern that we introduced as part of the *Updating variables* section. To update a list or one of its values, as we will learn in the next section, a line starting with a tilde (~) is needed.

Updating LIST values

While values, as shown in *Example 8*, can seemingly be shown, the output that was created was the name of the value, Monday, and not the string, "Monday". Regarding the output of a project, this is a small but important difference between a variable using the VAR keyword and those as part of a collection using the LIST keyword: only LIST values can be added to a list. To add a new value to an existing list, it must have been created by itself or another list:

Example 9 (Example9.ink):

```
LIST all_pets = Cats, Dogs, Fish
LIST current_pets = Cats, Dogs


~ current_pets = current_pets + Fish
```

In *Example 9*, the `Fish` value could be *added* to `current_pets` because it was created as part of another list, `all_pets`. This illustrates one of the major problems with using values from a list: while they can be very useful for introducing new possible values to a project, they must be defined before they can be accessed. Any new list is dependent on values that were previously defined or created within its assignment. However, it is possible to change the value to another type of data in ink:

Example 10 (Example10.ink):

```
LIST standing_with_family_members =
father = 0,
mother = 1,
sister = 2,
brother = 0
```

In *Example 10*, each of the values of the `standing_with_family_members` list is also assigned a number. This is allowed in ink and can be a useful way to create specific values of a list associated with numerical values in a project. However, accessing these numbers requires understanding another ink concept: **functions**.

Calling functions

Functions are a foundational part of most programming languages. In ink, a function is a subset of code that can accept input separated by commas, may produce output, and can be accessed through an operation called **calling**.

A function is *called* by using its name and then opening (`(`) and closing (`)`) parentheses. The operation of calling a function in ink temporarily moves the flow of the story to the code of a function and then returns it when the code finishes.

> **Note**
> Functions can only be called when used within code in ink. This means they either appear within opening and closing curly brackets or on lines starting with the tilde (~) as part of variable reassignment.

In this topic, we will start by reviewing some functions that are built into ink and how they can help us with common operations. Next, we will look at functions that have been designed to work exclusively with values created with the `LIST` keyword. These functions perform common operations on a list, such as letting us know the number of entries within it or picking a random entry from its collection.

Common mathematics functions

One of the most used functions in ink is RANDOM(). It accepts a minimum and a maximum whole number. It then picks a random number within the range specified.

For many role-playing games, a common need is a number within a certain range, such as between 1 and 4 or 1 and 20. The RANDOM() function allows us to set a range and then view the outcome:

Example 11 (Example11.ink):

```
An example of a dice roll of 1-to-20 is {RANDOM(1,20)}.
```

When the *Example 11* code is run, ink will encounter a set of curly brackets. It will then see the RANDOM() function with a minimum of 1 and a maximum of 20. Each time it is run, a different number in this range will be chosen:

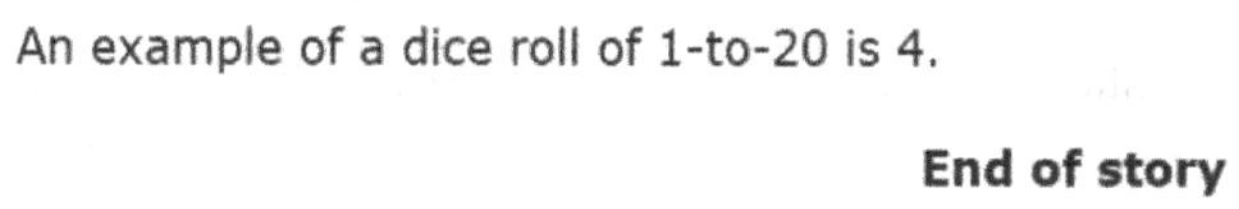

An example of a dice roll of 1-to-20 is 4.

End of story

Figure 4.5 – Screenshot of ink's output for Example 11

ink also has functions for converting between different types of numbers. The INT() function converts a decimal number into a whole (integer) number, while the FLOAT() function converts an integer into a decimal (float) number. Each accepts a single number and produces the output of a different type of number:

Example 12 (Example12.ink):

```
VAR example_decimal = 3.14
VAR example_integer = 5

Convert a decimal into an integer: {INT(example_decimal)}.
Convert an integer into a decimal: {FLOAT(example_integer +
    1.3)}.
```

The values that are produced by functions can be saved in variables. This allows, for example, the use of the RANDOM() function and its value, which has been saved as part of a variable:

Example 13 (Example13.ink):

```
A common table-top role-playing game combination is 2d6 where
two dice rolls of 1-to-6 are rolled, and their values combined.

VAR dice_one = 0
~ dice_one = RANDOM(1,6)
VAR dice_two = 0
~ dice_two = RANDOM(1,6)


The combined total of 2d6 is {dice_one + dice_two}.
```

The *Example 13* code contains two variables and two uses of the same function. As was mentioned at the start of the *Storing values using VAR* topic, variables must start with a static value. In the *Example 13* code, each variable is initially assigned a value of 0. They are immediately reassigned a value that's generated by the RANDOM() function. However, as part of the explicit rule with variables that are created using the VAR keyword, they must be set to a static value before they can be reassigned a dynamic variable that's been generated by a function such as RANDOM().

When run, the *Example 13* code creates the necessary variables and reassigns their values from a call to the RANDOM() function with a minimum of 1 and a maximum of 6. When ink encounters the text and use of curly brackets, it adds the two values:

A common table-top role-playing game combination is 2d6 where two dice rolls of 1-to-6 are rolled and their values combined.

The combined total of 2d6 is 10.

End of story

Figure 4.6 – Screenshot of ink's output for Example 13

Reminder

Like using a shuffle alternative and the VAR keyword, the output of the RANDOM() function cannot be used as the initial value of a variable. It must be created first, and then reassigned the value produced by RANDOM().

As we have seen, there are multiple built-in functions in ink for working with single values. This is also true of values that are created using the LIST keyword. In the next section, we will review some of the functions that have been designed specifically for lists and their values.

Using LIST functions

While there are functions that have been designed for a single value, most built-in functions in ink are used with a list. These all start with the LIST_ prefix and have the action or operation they perform or access as the second word. For example, to count the number of included values within a list, the LIST_COUNT() function can be used:

Example 14 (Example14.ink):

```
LIST days_of_week =
Monday,
Tuesday,
Wednesday,
Thursday,
Friday,
Saturday,
Sunday

The total days are {LIST_COUNT(days_of_week)}.
```

When run, the *Example 14* code creates a list containing seven values. In the curly brackets is a call to the LIST_COUNT() function. This function is then passed the days_of_week list. Based on the lines that were used in the assignment of the list, the default assumption would be that the output will be 7 based on the number of days in the list. However, this is not the case. Its output is 0:

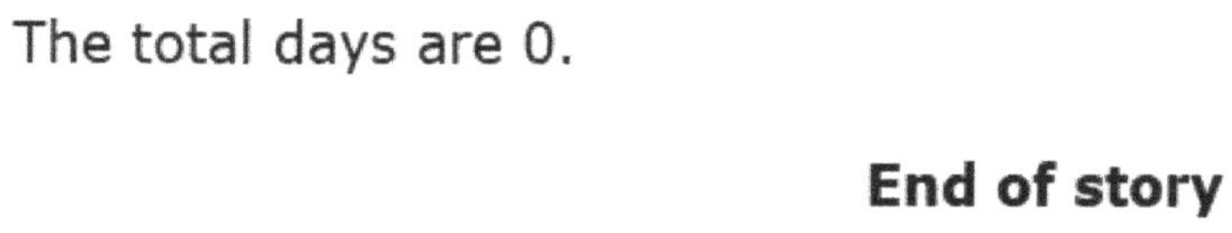

The total days are 0.

End of story

Figure 4.7 – Screenshot of ink's output for Example 14

The output produced by *Example 14* shows a hidden aspect of working with values from a list. Technically, all the values for creating a list are known as a **Boolean set** in ink. Each value that's created by a list is set to either `true` or `false` and by default, all values are set to `false`.

The use of the `LIST_COUNT()` function *counts* the number of `true` values within the list. In *Example 14*, there are none. The count that was produced by the function is correct. To change a value from its default of `false` to `true`, it needs to be enclosed in opening (`(`) and closing (`)`) parentheses:

Example 15 (Example15.ink):

```
LIST days_of_week =
(Monday),
(Tuesday),
(Wednesday),
(Thursday),
(Friday),
(Saturday),
(Sunday)

The total days are {LIST_COUNT(days_of_week)}.
```

In *Example 15*, the output includes the number 7. This is correct. Each value within the list from *Example 14* is now enclosed within its own set of parentheses, changing its value from `false` to `true` for each.

For the cases where every value, regardless of being `true` or `false`, is wanted from a list, the `LIST_ALL()` function returns *all* values:

Example 16 (Example16.ink):

```
LIST days_of_week =
(Monday),
(Tuesday),
(Wednesday),
(Thursday),
(Friday),
(Saturday),
(Sunday)
```

```
The days of the week are: {LIST_ALL(days_of_week)}.
```

In *Example 16*, the use of the `LIST_ALL()` function returns all the values that are currently part of the `days_of_week` list:

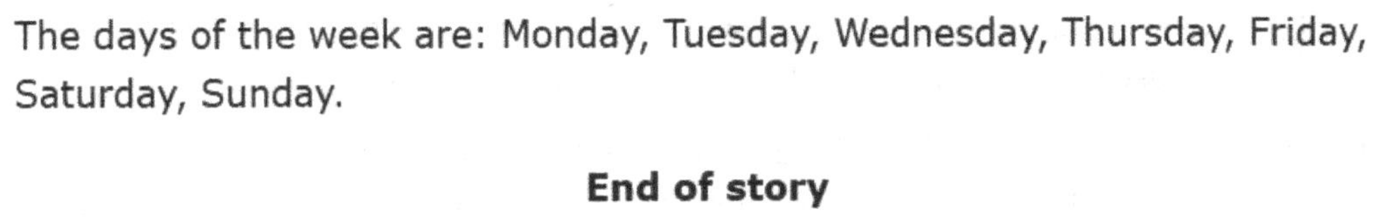

The days of the week are: Monday, Tuesday, Wednesday, Thursday, Friday, Saturday, Sunday.

End of story

Figure 4.8 – Screenshot of ink's output for Example 16

The `LIST_RANDOM()` function returns a random entry regarding the total number of `true` values in a list, as shown in the following example:

Example 17 (Example17.ink):

```
LIST days_of_week =
(Monday),
(Tuesday),
(Wednesday),
Thursday,
Friday,
Saturday,
Sunday

A random day of the week is: {LIST_RANDOM(days_of_week)}.
```

In *Example 17*, only the Monday, Tuesday, and Wednesday values are set to `true`. The other values of `days_of_week`, because they are set to `false` by default, cannot be accessed by `LIST_RANDOM()`.

Returning to the code from *Example 10*, the `LIST_VALUE()` function can be used to access any data that's been assigned to a value as part of a list:

Example 18 (Example18.ink):

```
LIST standing_with_family_members =
father = 0,
```

```
mother = 1,
sister = 2,
brother = 0

The value of sister is {LIST_VALUE(sister)}.
```

In this improved version of *Example 10*, known as *Example 18*, the LIST_VALUE() function can be used to access the data that's been assigned to the sister value.

While ink has many functions for performing different options, both mathematically and with the values of a list, it also provides authors with the ability to create their own. In the next topic, we will review how to create and call functions.

Making new functions and calling knots

The *Calling functions* topic introduced functions for accepting input, possibly producing output, and explained how ink's built-in functions can be called.

It is also possible to create new functions in ink using the function keyword. Any new functions created in ink can be used like any others, and they are often a useful way to create separate lines of code that can be used across a project or multiple times without the need to write the same code again.

In this topic, we will explore how to create new functions using the function keyword. We will learn how they can be called, perform a small task, and even potentially return data. In *Chapter 2, Knots, Diverts, and Looping Patterns*, we discussed knots initially. Different sections of a story are defined by a name. In ink, functions, as we will learn, are special types of knots. This relationship means knots can also be *called* and *passed* data.

A function is created in ink using at least two equals signs (=), the function keyword, the name of the function, and then the opening (() and closing ()) parentheses, which are put around its input (if any). The name of a function follows the same rules as variables and knots: they can contain numbers, letters, and an underscore character. They cannot contain other special symbols or spaces.

Like variables, functions are also *global* in ink. They can be accessed by any other code within the project once they have been created. Because both variables and functions are global, a common pattern is to design a function that changes a single variable. This allows an author to define an action that takes place when calling the function, such as increasing or decreasing its current value:

Example 19 (Example19.ink):

```
VAR money = 30
VAR apples = 0
VAR oranges = 0
You approach the marketplace and consider what is on sale.
-> market

== market
You have {money} gold.
You have purchased {apples} apples.
You have purchased {oranges} oranges.

+ {money > 10} [Buy Apple for 10 gold]
    ~ decreaseMoney(10)
    ~ increaseApples()
    -> market
+ {money > 15} [Buy Oranges for 15 gold]
    ~ decreaseMoney(15)
    ~ increaseOranges()
    -> market
* [Leave market]
    -> DONE

== function decreaseMoney(amount)
~ money = money - amount

== function increaseApples()
~ apples = apples + 1
```

```
== function increaseOranges()
~ oranges = oranges + 1
```

Example 19 uses three different functions. The first, decreaseMoney(), accepts a value called amount. This is an example of a **parameter**. When creating a function, different variables can be defined within its open and closing parentheses. These are known as its *parameters*, and they affect how it performs calculations or processes.

When a function is called, the data that's passed to it is called its **arguments**. These match its parameters. The values that are passed as arguments become the values of its parameters. *Example 19* uses one function, decreaseMoney(), that has a parameter and receives a single argument, and two functions, increaseApples() and increaseOranges(), that do not accept arguments.

The placement of the increaseApples() and increaseOranges() functions also matches a common pattern in ink where functions for adjusting the values of variables are found at the bottom of the code. Because both are global, which means they can be accessed from anywhere in the project, functions can be defined anywhere in the project.

However, functions, like their sister concept knots, define themselves as being all the lines between when they start and the next knot or function. Placing them at the bottom of a file prevents issues where code might be confused or considered part of another knot or function.

Functions are not the only concepts able to define parameters and accept arguments. In ink, **knots** can also be called as if they were functions. This is because functions are special types of knots that can return data. This also marks the difference between them. A knot can accept data, but only a function can return data. However, using knots in this way allows us to easily track values within a looping structure:

Example 20 (Example20.ink):

```
-> time_machine(RANDOM(20,80))
== time_machine(loop)
The large machine looms over everything in the room. With
flashing lights, odd wires running between parts, and a
presence all its own, it seems to be almost a living, pulsating
thing as the scientist runs between sections parts and adjusts
various parts.
"I'm so close!" he shouts as he turns a knob and then pulls
down a lever. "I just need more time to figure out how to
control the loops!"
```

```
You regard him and the machine skeptically.

"If you could, just press that last button and everything
should be all set for the first demonstration of my time
machine! I'm so glad the newspaper sent you to cover this
event," he says, adjusting more settings on the grand machine
in front of you.

You pause to try to understand the blinking lights as he yells
again. "Press the button for me! I just need to make some last-
minute changes over here."

On the panel in front of you is a large, green button. You
consider it and the scientist rushing around across the room.

+ [Press button]
    ~ loop = loop + 1
    There is a flash of light and the readings on the
      machine show a message: "This is loop {loop}."
    -> time_machine(loop)
```

There is a single variable within *Example 20* that's created as a parameter of the time_
machine knot. Before the loop starts, the RANDOM() function is used to select a value
within the range of 20 to 80. This value is passed to the knot in the first loop. Whenever
the player selects the **Press button** option, the loop value is increased by one and its
current value is passed to the time_machine knot. On any future loops, the loop
variable is increased by one, and it sends its current value into the next loop.

The code in *Example 20* also shows how variables can be used without the VAR keyword.
Within the knot, the loop variable exists as a parameter. This means it exists as a variable,
but only within the time_machine knot. When used in this way, the loop variable will
not be global. As a part of the time_machine knot, the loop variable cannot be used
outside of its code.

Functions are a powerful concept in ink. However, they do have two major limitations
compared to working with knots. The first is that functions cannot use choices of any
kind. Functions cannot branch a story and must *return* to where they were called when
they are finished. The second limitation is that functions cannot divert to another section
of a story. Like the first limitation, a function should only perform a small task or change
a value.

Calling knots as if they were functions can be very useful for many projects. However, unlike functions, knots cannot return values. As shown in *Example 20*, it is possible to use knots for some, but not all, of the same purposes as functions in ink. Authors must consider whether a function or a knot is a better way to complete a task or present information. If the goal is to process data and return a value, a function is best. If data is to be passed, options must be presented, or the story may divert in some way, a knot is the better way to organize your code and data.

Summary

In this chapter, we learned more about how variables work, and how they can be created using the VAR keyword. With multiple types of data, variables must be created using static values. They can then be changed through an operation called assignment using lines starting with a tilde (~) for writing a single line of code.

In the second topic, for the cases where we needed multiple values, we saw that the LIST keyword can be used. This keyword allows us to create values other variables can use, but also comes with the limitations that only values created with LIST can be used with a list. We also examined how all the values of a list are part of a Boolean set and have either true or false values upon creation.

Next, in the third topic, we investigated how functions work in ink. With several built-in functions, we can create random numbers or convert between types of numbers. With LIST values, we compared the results of LIST_COUNT() and LIST_ALL() by examining how to change the values of a list from true to false when they are created.

Finally, in the last topic, we wrote some functions with the function keyword to perform simple tasks, such as adjusting the value of a variable. Because both variables were created using the VAR keyword and functions are global, we saw that a common pattern is to use a function to change the value of a variable. As part of this topic, we also revisited knots and learned that functions are special types of knots. This allows both to receive data using parameters, though only a function can return data.

As we will see in the coming chapters on combining ink and Unity, understanding how values are stored and accessed in ink will be vital to creating a unified project. We must understand how ink works with different values across both those created using the VAR keyword and the LIST keyword before we can work with code in Unity. By understanding the relationship between variables and functions, we can begin to write ink code and, much later, run it alongside C# code in Unity.

In the next chapter, *Chapter 5, Tunnels and Threads*, we will look at the last two major concepts in ink: **tunnels** and **threads**. Using many of the concepts introduced over the last four chapters, we will use tunnels to create advanced structures in ink with very little code. With threads, we will break up a digital story into even more parts and have ink combine everything for us as a reader is diverted from one knot to another. This will create an intricate narrative experience based on understanding and managing story flow between sections of a story.

Questions

1. What is the operation called where a variable gets a value?

2. What is the operation called when a string is created by "adding" two other strings or a string and a number together?

3. How is the tilde (~) used with variables and code in ink?

4. What kind of set are the values of a list?

5. What is the technical term for a variable that's created as part of a function or knot and defined within its parentheses?

5
Tunnels and Threads

This chapter begins with the concept of a **tunnel**. Created using multiple diverts and at least two knots (please refer to *Chapter 2, Knots, Diverts, and Looping Patterns*), tunnels serve as a faster way in which to create complex structures than previously discussed in the last chapters. Following this, we will move on to review **threads**, which is another way of using diverts to connect multiple parts of an ink project dynamically. Finally, we will look at combining tunnels and threads to make even more complex structures based on the simple rules of how ink understands knots and diverts within a story.

In this chapter, we will cover the following main topics:

- Diverting to a divert
- Pulling on threads
- Combining tunnels and threads

In this chapter, we will explore the various ways of using tunnels and threads to make more complex projects. We have already explored multiple levels of choices and their outcomes to create a subdivided story. Instead of diverting to one knot or stitch after another, we will learn how to integrate tunnels as a series of diverts before returning to their original location. We will also look at how knots can be easily combined into one by *threading* them together.

Technical requirements

The examples used in this chapter, in the `*.ink` files, can be found on GitHub at `https://github.com/PacktPublishing/Dynamic-Story-Scripting-with-the-ink-Scripting-Language/tree/main/Chapter5`.

Diverting to a divert

In *Chapter 2, Knots, Diverts, and Looping Patterns*, the concept of a divert was introduced alongside story sections called knots. Using diverts and knots, looping structures were created and other ink concepts were also revealed as alternatives (please refer to *Chapter 3, Sequences, Cycles, and Shuffling Text*). The use of functions and passing values to knots were covered in *Chapter 4, Variables, Lists, and Functions*. This section builds on those concepts by explaining how diverts can be used to create more advanced stories.

In *Chapter 2, Knots, Diverts, and Looping Patterns*, diverts appeared according to the following pattern:

Example 1:

```
For the reader, <>
-> next_part
== next_part
this appears as one line.
-> DONE
```

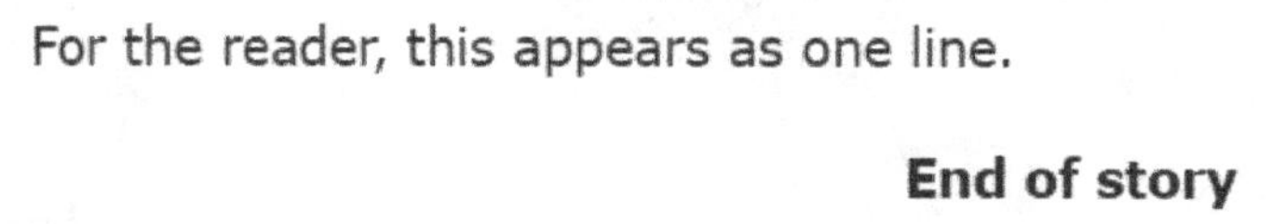

For the reader, this appears as one line.

End of story

Figure 5.1 – Inky's output for Example 1

A divert can also be used multiple times. In ink, this is known as the concept of a **tunnel**. The flow will move to a knot and then back to its original position. From the reader's perspective, the flow *tunnels* from one section to another. Tunnels are an incredibly useful concept in ink where looping structures are common.

In this topic, we will review how to make and use tunnels. Instead of needing to specify each location of a divert within a knot or a stitch, a tunnel allows an author to move the flow of a story through a series of sections and then back again when the tunnel finally ends.

Making tunnels

Tunnels are created in ink by using a divert, ->, the name of a knot or stitch, and then another divert, ->. This signals to ink that the flow will move to the knot and then back again. In the destination knot, two diverts are then used together: ->->. This creates the *tunneling* effect of the flow moving to the knot and then moving back again:

Example 2:

```
For the reader, <>
-> next_part ->
<> as one line
== next_part
this appears
->->
```

Example 2 can appear confusing if you don't remember how the flow works in ink. A divert moves the flow to a destination in the story. In *Example 2*, the flow starts with the text of For the reader, <>. Then, this is diverted to the next_part knot. The start of the tunnel begins with the code of -> next_part ->, continues into the next_part knot, and then returns with the use of two diverts, ->->. For a reader who only sees the output, it will appear as a complete sentence:

For the reader, this appears as one line

End of story

Figure 5.2 – Inky's output from Example 2

Reminder

Chapter 1, Text, Flow, Choices, and Weaves, introduced the concept
of glue and the use of the less-than and greater-than symbols together.
This concept *glues* one line to the end of the previous. In *Example 2,* glue is
used before the start of the tunnel and then after it ends to create the complete
sentence from the knot in the story.

Tunnels can connect any two points within a story. In *Example 2*, the tunnel started, moved to a knot, and then returned. Another use of a tunnel might be to create a series of story events for a player to view. You can do this by creating a tunnel from one knot to the next until the end of the story:

Example 3:

```
You lift the body onto your back and then carry it over to the
edge of the hole before dropping it again. You watch it hit the
ground with a pleasant thump. It is dirty work, gravedigging
is (you laugh at your own joke as you brush some dirt off
your hands and onto your already dirty pants), but it pays the
bills.
```

```
-> past -> present -> future -> DONE
```

```
== past
```
```
You did not want to be a gravedigger at first. Who does? No,
you stumbled into it as many people do. You needed the money
and dead people were dead as far as you were concerned. Dig a
hole, put the body in, cover the hole. Easy work. Easy money.
```
```
->->
```

```
== present
```
```
You shake your head and then kick the body so that it plops
into the grave. Another sound you did not expect to like when
you started so many years ago, but you take little joys where
you can. Life is funny that way.
```
```
->->
```

```
== future
```
```
"There's no future in the dead," your wife had said. But she
is dead now, too. And what did she know? Other than dirt! (You
laugh at another of your jokes.)
```
```
You pick up the shovel.
```
```
One load of dirt after another.
```
```
It is a living. Or a dying! (You laugh again to yourself as you
continue.)
```
```
->->
```

In *Example 3*, the three different knots (that is, past, present, and future) are all part of one long tunnel. The first connects to the past knot, the past knot is then connected to the present knot, the present knot is connected to the future knot, and, finally, the future knot is connected to the DONE knot to end the flow and the story. In each of these cases, the use of the two diverts, ->->, points back to where the tunnel started before it continues to the next knot in the longer series. As with *Example 2* and its complete sentence, the resulting output from *Example 3* is one single flow through the sections to create a complete narrative experience for the reader.

Tunneling to tunnels

Example 3 pointed towards a great use of tunnels: they can connect to other tunnels! It is possible to tunnel into a tunnel in ink. While linear patterns such as the one used in *Example 3* are common, advanced patterns reuse tunnels as part of larger, looping structures. Because knots that use two diverts will always return to where they started, it is possible to use knots to perform small calculations or to check values before continuing the repeating pattern:

Example 4:

```
VAR playful = 0
VAR anger = 0
On your daily walk, you decide to sit for a few minutes on a
nearby bench. You close your eyes to take in the evening sun.
Suddenly, you hear a small sound and look down. A kitten is
circling your legs.
-> kitten
== kitten
-> check_kitten ->
+ [Scratch the kitten on its head]
    You pet the kitten on its head.
    -> scratch_head -> kitten
+ [Scratch the kitten on its side]
    You pet the kitten on its side.
    -> scratch_side -> kitten
== scratch_head
~ playful = playful + 1
->->
== scratch_side
```

```
~ anger = anger + 1
->->
== check_kitten
{anger >= 2: The kitten seems angry and walks away. -> DONE}
{playful >= 2: One moment, you were scratching the kitten and
the next your hand has some small cuts on it. You decide to
leave the kitten alone. -> DONE}
->->
```

Example 4 demonstrates a more complex pattern using knots, variables, and tunnels. For each loop of the kitten knot, a tunnel is created for the check_kitten knot, which then returns to kitten again. In the check_kitten knot, two checks are made. The first check is to make sure the value of the anger variable is greater than or equal to 2. If it is, the sentence is shown and then the story diverts to DONE. The second check is to make sure the playful variable is greater than or equal to 2. If this second check is true, a different sentence is shown, and the story diverts to DONE. Inside the weave created by the two sticky choices, each option, either **Scratch the kitten on its head** or **scratch the kitten on its side**, diverts to a tunnel to either of the two knots: scratch_head or scratch_side. Inside each, the knots associated with the player's actions increase the value of the variable.

Example 4 uses multiple tunnels to create a complex pattern. However, there is another concept in ink that would make the same code easier to understand: **threads**. As we will discuss in the next section, threads allow us to easily pull in knots without needing to divert to them first.

Pulling on threads

Diverts were introduced as *pointing* to their destination. To create a tunnel, a hyphen and a greater-than symbol were combined, - >, on either side of the name of the knot or stitch. However, diverts can *point* inward as well. When a divert is created with a less-than symbol and a hyphen, < -, it becomes a different concept called a **thread**. Instead of moving the flow to the destination, ink *threads* the destination's text or code into another location.

In this section, we will work with threads to collapse more complex weaves into simpler structures. Instead of multiple levels of choices and their text outcomes, we will use threads to achieve the same result in a more efficient way.

Making threads

Often, threads are considered to be an inverse of diverts. Instead of the flow moving to the section of the story, the section of the story moves to the current position of the flow. Returning to the code from *Example 4*, threads can be used in multiple places to achieve the same result:

Example 5:

```
VAR playful = 0
VAR anger = 0
On your daily walk, you decide to sit for a few minutes on a
nearby bench. You close your eyes to take in the evening sun.
Suddenly, you hear a small sound and look down. A kitten is
circling your legs.
-> kitten
== kitten
<- check_kitten
+ [Scratch the kitten on its head]
    You pet the kitten on its head.
    <- scratch head
    -> kitten
+ [Scratch kitten on its side]
    You pet the kitten on its side.
    <- scratch_side
    -> kitten
== scratch_head
~ playful = playful + 1
== scratch_side
~ anger = anger + 1
== check_kitten
{anger >= 2: The kitten seems angry and walks away. -> DONE}
{playful >= 2: One moment, you were scratching the kitten and
the next your hand has some small cuts on it. You decide to
leave the kitten alone. -> DONE}
```

In *Example 5*, threads are used in place of the previous tunnels in *Example 4*. The `scratch_head` and `scratch_side` knots are now *threaded* into the code of the `kitten` knot. This is also true for `check_kitten`. Instead of creating multiple tunnels, threads are often used to collapse an increasingly complex structure into sections that can be *threaded* together.

> **Warning**
>
> Sometimes, the use of complex tunnel and thread structures can confuse Inky. Always double-check all of the code when using these more advanced concepts!

Using multiple threads

Each use of a thread must be on its own line. The reason why they cannot be combined is that ink moves the section of the story up to the location of the current flow. A second thread cannot have its content moved to the previous location. It no longer exists! However, threads, like diverts, can also be elements within a set or alternative. Just as a different form of a divert can be *pointing* inward, threads can be used with a shuffle on a single line:

Example 6:

```
"Hey! Jesse!" you shout, trying to get her attention. Hearing
your voice, she turns, and you hurry to catch up with her as
you jog from the building after your class.
{~ <- question_one|<- question_two}
== question_one
<> "How was your class"? you ask.
== question_two
<> "Are you going to the party tonight?" you ask.
```

In *Example 6*, threads are used as elements of a shuffle. Each time the story is run, one of the two threads will be chosen and *threaded* into the story, creating a new experience. Combining threads with alternatives in this way is useful when creating *alternative* content for a story that is accessed as part of the thread itself.

A common pattern found in many role-playing video games uses various player statistics to determine what content is available based on testing the value of a variable. If it is within a certain range, content can then be *threaded* into the current weave. This will add additional context for the result of an action for the reader:

Example 7:

```
VAR strength = 16
VAR intelligence = 16
-> save_or_doom

== save_or_doom
The villain holds the ancient artifact and is moments away
from enslaving the world with its limitless power as part of a
complex ritual.
* {strength > 15} [Use strength]
    <- use_strength
* {intelligence > 15} [Use intelligence]
    <- use_intelligence
- -> DONE

= use_strength
You throw your hand axe as hard as you can. It strikes the
artifact, shattering it into multiple pieces and ending the
ritual.

= use_intelligence
You quickly calculate the size of the artifact based on its
materials and cast the spell to banish it to another dimension.
In a blink of an eye, the ritual ends!
```

Each of the stitches in *Example 7* holds additional text. Because the stitches are a part of the overall save_or_doom knot, they can be used as part of a thread. Subsections of a story are still *sections*.

Example 7 also uses conditional options, as covered in *Chapter 2, Knots, Diverts, and Looping Patterns*, and variables, as discussed in *Chapter 4, Variables, Lists, and Functions*. By testing for the range of values of the `strength` and `intelligence` variables, the **Use strength** or **Use intelligence** options are shown to the reader. In *Example 7*, because both variables have values greater than `15`, both options are shown:

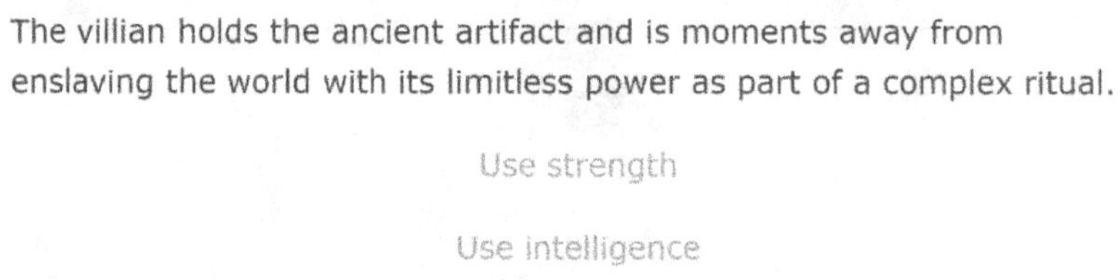

> The villian holds the ancient artifact and is moments away from
> enslaving the world with its limitless power as part of a complex ritual.
>
> Use strength
>
> Use intelligence

Figure 5.3 – Inky's output from Example 7

A single thread can be created using the inverse action of diverting. Instead of moving to a location, the section moves to the current moment in the flow. Additionally, multiple threads can be combined to create a continuous narrative experience for the reader as they are pulled together. When working with threads, there is one more important aspect: the DONE keyword. In the last section of this topic, we will examine how threads can be closed and what this means when you are using threads inside each other.

Ending threads

The DONE and END keywords were introduced in *Chapter 2, Knots, Diverts, and Looping Patterns*. The differences between the two keywords were explained in their usage. The END keyword stops the story, and the DONE keyword stops the current flow. When using threads, the flow of a story is also affected. In other words, the DONE keyword closes the *current* flow. In many cases, this will be the story itself. When using threads, the keyword closes the thread itself.

When creating knots in Inky, often, authors will get a warning suggesting the DONE keyword is needed within a knot that does not contain the keyword. When working with threads, this warning clues the author into this important aspect of threads and the DONE keyword:

Example 8:

```
<- thread_1
<- thread_2
== thread_1
* This is a choice
-> DONE
```

```
== thread_2
* This is another choice
-> DONE
```

Example 8 uses two instances of the DONE keyword. This might seem strange, but each use of the keyword closes its own thread. When run within Inky, the two choices, each within a separate thread, will be combined:

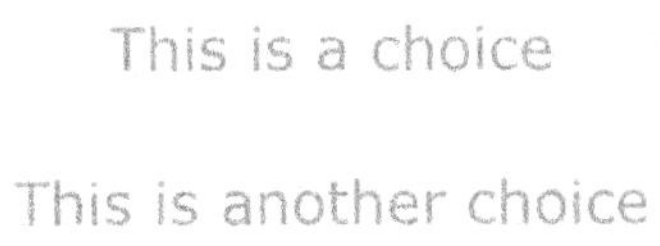

This is a choice

This is another choice

Figure 5.4 – The combined thread output for Example 8

In *Example 8*, the separate uses of the DONE keyword do not interact with each other. Each thread is contained within itself. This becomes evident when trying to move the inclusion of the second thread inside the first after the DONE keyword:

Example 9:

```
<- thread_1
== thread_1
* This is a choice
-> DONE
<- thread_2
== thread_2
* This is another choice
-> DONE
```

In *Example 9*, the second thread comes after the use of the DONE keyword. Unlike *Example 8*, where both choices will be combined into a single weave, the story will end before the second thread occurs:

This is a choice

Figure 5.5 – Thread closing in Example 9

Example 9 demonstrates the interaction between the DONE keyword and the threads. The DONE keyword closes the current flow. In *Example 9*, the second thread inside the first is never reached because it is closed using the DONE keyword.

Threads and tunnels are not separate concepts, but two different ways in which to achieve similar results based on the needs of the author. In the next topic, we will look at various ways of combining both concepts to create even more complex stories. We will use tunnels to move to a location in a story and examine how threads can be repeated instead of writing more code.

Combining tunnels and threads

Tunnels allow the flow of a story to move to a knot or a stitch and then return. Threads act as the inverse, moving the content from the knot or the stitch to the current flow position. Together, they form a powerful way in which to craft a story composed of different parts. Often, in advanced projects, these two concepts are paired together with weaves and gathering points to expand or contract the number of possible branches.

Tunnels can be reused, and threads can be repeated. In this topic, we will explore how threads and tunnels can be combined to create more complex stories using less overall code.

Reusing tunnels and repeating threads

Example 4 used multiple tunnels, and *Example 5* showed the same result using multiple threads. It is also possible to combine multiple tunnels and threads by breaking up content into stitches as part of multiple knots for each part of a story. For example, many role-playing video games start by presenting dialogue from a character. Then, they provide the player with the illusion of control by letting them choose between various options before, finally, looping back to the same options until the player makes a certain selection to continue:

Example 10:

```
VAR has_rake = false


-> tutorial
== tutorial
= awake
You feel a hand on your shoulder and wake up to a young woman
frowning down at you.
Jane: "I see you are finally awake! I wish you would stop
sleeping under this tree instead of working."
```

```
Jane: "Uncle John is going to catch you one of these days and
then you will be in trouble."
Jane: "Do you remember what you need to do today?"
* [What was it again?]
    <- tasks
* [I remember.]
    <- remember
- -> rake ->
-> old_shrine
= tasks
Jane: "In case you forgot, you need to clean up all the leaves
around the old shrine."
Jane: "And don't forget to take your rake!"
= remember
Jane: "Good! Get out to that old shrine and finish your
cleaning!"
= rake
+ [Pick up rake]
    ~ has_rake = true
+ [Skip the rake]
    ~ has_rake = false
- ->->
== old_shrine
{has_rake == false: You realize you do not have your rake.}
+ {has_rake == false} [Retrieve rake]
    -> tutorial.rake ->
    {has_rake == false: -> old_shrine}
- You begin to rake the leaves around the old shrine.
-> DONE
```

Example 10 reuses a tunnel. The first instance occurs when the reader selects between
the **What was it again?** and **I remember.** options. When the reader encounters the
old_shrine knot and does not have the rake (that is, if has_rake is equal to false),
they are prompted with the **Retrieve rake** option and the second possible instance of
the tunnel.

Threads are used in *Example 10* to break up the text of the responses from the character. This creates a simplified weave with the text split into its stitches. For authors, this pattern allows them to change or add to the response text without needing to worry about the code portion of the weave.

Finally, gathering points (as discussed in *Chapter 1, Text, Flow, Choices, and Weaves*) are used three times. The first one collapses the possible branches of the first weave and creates the first instance of a tunnel. The second occurs as part of the `rake` stitch. This gathering point is the end of both instances of tunnels and collapses the result of either option: **Pick up rake** or **Skip the rake**. The last gathering point occurs at the very end of the story. Once the player has their rake (that is, `has_rake` is equal to `true`), the **Retrieve rake** option no longer appears, and the story ends with the character raking the leaves at the old shrine.

Dialogue tags are used multiple times in *Example 10*. When writing dialogue coming from a particular character, a *tag* can be used to specify who is saying the words. Often, these tags will appear with the character's name and their action after the dialogue, such as `"This is an example,"` `Dan wrote`. However, in *Example 8*, the name of the character appears before the dialogue to signal who is saying the words. *Chapter 10, Dialogue Systems with ink*, will revisit the use of tags and examine some approaches for writing and tagging dialogue appearing in a video game.

Threads with tunnels

Threads move a section of a story to the current flow position when moving through the in-memory version of the code. Internally, this does not change their actual location in the larger story code but their connection to the current version of the flow as the story is run. This means it is possible to include a tunnel inside a thread. In these scenarios, the flow would *thread* the knot or stitch and then move to another section and back again:

Example 11:

```
<- knot_example.stitch_one
<- knot_example.stitch_two


== knot_example
= stitch_one
-> tunnel ->
= stitch_two
-> tunnel ->
== tunnel
```

```
This is a tunnel inside a thread!
->->
```

Example 11 demonstrates the basic pattern of using tunnels inside threads. This is safe to do in ink because of the way the flow *threads* through the knots or stitches. A more complicated usage might be part of a dialogue system for a video game, where data is passed to knots to perform different small calculations as part of the reaction to a player following certain branches of a conversation:

Example 12:

```
VAR reputation = 10
-> villager_1
== villager_1
Villager: Heroes! You have returned from fighting the monsters
in the forest! Did you find any sign of my husband? He has been
missing for several days.
+ \(Lie\) We have not found him yet.
    <- adjust_reputation(-10)
+ We found what was left of him. I'm sorry to report he is
  dead.
    <- adjust_reputation(10)
+ I used his leg to fight off some spiders! Oh. Right...
  he's, you know, dead.
    <- adjust_reputation(-15)
- -> DONE
== adjust_reputation(amount)
~ reputation = reputation + amount
-> report_reputation ->
== report_reputation
Current reputation: {reputation}
```

Example 12 is a more practical example of the pattern introduced in *Example 1*. It uses a thread to pass data to a knot as if it was a function. Additionally, *Example 12* uses a tunnel inside the `adjust_reputation` knot as a connection to the `report_reputation` knot. For each choice, the value of the `reputation` variable will be changed after a reader makes the selection. The new value of `reputation` will be shown as a result.

> **Note**
> *Example 12* uses a backslash, \, with opening, (, and closing,), parentheses.
> These *escape* the use of the parentheses instead of creating an optional label.

Summary

In this chapter, we learned even more about how diverts work with knots and stitches in ink. We explored how the concept of a tunnel connects two different sections in ink. When a story runs, the flow moves to the knot or the stitch and then returns with the use of two diverts, - > - >. We also reviewed how tunnels can be used as part of a more complicated flow pattern of a longer series of connections between two sections. Next, we saw how threads, another concept in ink, act as the inverse of a divert, where a section is moved to the current flow location instead of the flow moving to its content. Finally, we examined some patterns of using tunnels inside threads to pass data to a knot and show the changed values of a variable.

Threads and tunnels, while more advanced concepts, create simpler overall code. Threads allow developers to separate code into different sections and then *thread* them back together again. Tunnels allow developers to achieve the same general result as threads but in a different way. Instead of pulling content together, a tunnel moves to a knot or a stitch and then back again, *tunneling* through a story to a location and then back again. Threads and tunnels have their specific usages, but both allow a developer to create more complex projects by using their different sections more efficiently.

In the next chapter, we move on to use the ink-Unity Integration plugin. While Inky has been used to show the ink code output, the ink-Unity Integration plugin will allow us to have far more control over how an ink story runs. In the coming chapters, we will also learn how to use C# and the ink API to make selections, change the value of variables, and even access functions in ink code.

Questions

1. To return from a tunnel in a knot or a stitch, which ink concept must be used twice?
2. How do tunnels work in ink?
3. How are threads different from diverts and tunnels?
4. Can multiple threads be used on the same line?

Section 2:
ink Unity API

By the time you've completed this section, you will be able to make choices and access internal values in an ink story using the ink-Unity Integration plugin in Unity. This section contains the following chapters:

- *Chapter 6, Adding and Working with the ink-Unity Integration Plugin*
- *Chapter 7, Unity API – Making Choices and Story Progression*
- *Chapter 8, Story API – Accessing ink Variables and Functions*
- *Chapter 9, Story API – Observing and Reacting to Story Events*

6
Adding and Working with the ink-Unity Integration Plugin

This chapter begins with discussing how to add the **ink-Unity Integration** plugin to existing projects in Unity. We will then discuss working with ink files, `.ink`, and their compiled forms, `.json`, within a Unity project and its Project window. Then, we will review how to associate Inky with ink source files and use it to edit files directly from Unity. Finally, we will conclude by examining how to adjust the plugin's settings for a project.

In this chapter, we are going to cover the following main topics:

- Adding the ink-Unity Integration plugin
- Working with ink files
- Adjusting plugin settings

In this chapter, we will find, import, and work with the ink-Unity Integration plugin. This will allow us to work with ink files and adjust the plugin settings. We cannot work with ink files without the plugin, and the steps outlined in this chapter will help developers set up the package for later chapters focused on working with ink files and the Story API available after installing the plugin.

Note on Unity versions

This chapter has been tested with **Unity 2020.3 (LTS)** and **Unity 2021.1 (current)**. This chapter also covers *version 1.0.2* of the **ink-Unity Integration** plugin. Inkle reports that *version 1.0.2* of the ink-Unity Integration plugin is compatible with *2018.4* and later versions of Unity, but only *2020.3 (LTS)* and *2021.1 (current)* are recommended.

Technical requirements

The examples used in this chapter, in `*.ink` files, can be found online on GitHub: `https://github.com/PacktPublishing/Dynamic-Story-Scripting-with-the-ink-Scripting-Language/tree/main/Chapter6`.

Adding the ink-Unity Integration plugin

We cannot work with Ink files in Unity without a special package called the **ink-Unity Integration** plugin. Like other packages for Unity, it can only be added to an existing project and must be re-imported for any new project wanting to use its code and available API. In this topic, we will work through the steps required to find, import, and verify the plugin is ready for use in a project. Each section in this topic should be used with the same project as the first section, *Finding and importing the plugin*, beginning with instructions to create a new Unity project based on the 2D template.

Note

The official name of the package is ink-Unity Integration. However, Inkle, the creators of ink, call this package a *plugin* in its own documentation. This book follows the same naming convention to avoid confusion.

Finding and importing the plugin

The process for finding and importing the ink-Unity Integration plugin requires the following steps:

1. Create a new Unity project using the built-in 2D template.

> **Warning**
>
> **Inkle** does not recommend using the Unity Asset Store version of the ink-Unity Integration plugin because of the delays between updates. This book will use the installation method recommended by the developers of the plugin to get the most up-to-date version.

2. Navigate to the **OpenUPM** page for the ink-Unity Integration plugin: `https://openupm.com/packages/com.inklestudios.ink-unity-integration/`.

3. Click on the **Get installer.unitypackage** link on the right-hand side:

Figure 6.1 – OpenUPM page for the ink-Unity Integration plugin

4. Clicking on the **Get installer.unitypackage** link will prompt a file download. Once the download finishes, find the local file and run the installer.

5. Open the downloaded installer file while Unity is open. This will open the **Import Unity Package** window in Unity and load the contents of the installer file.

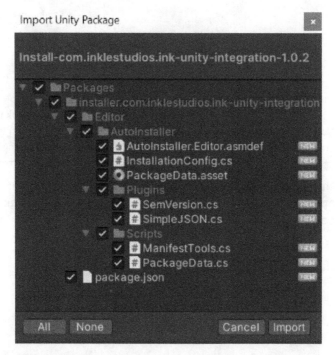

Figure 6.2 – Import Unity Package window showing ink-Unity Integration

6. In the **Import Unity Package** window, click on **All** and then **Import**. This will guarantee all files are selected and imported. Once the importing is done, Unity will give a message that a new scoped registry has been added to the project.

Figure 6.3 – Importing a scoped registry window in Unity

7. Click the **Close** button to close the **Importing a scoped registry** window. Unity also opened the **Project Settings** window. This can be closed as well.

As one final step, we will test that the package is installed and ready for use. In the next section, we will work with the **Package Manager** window.

Verifying the package is installed

Depending on the version of Unity, other packages in use, or developer settings, it can sometimes be unclear whether the ink-Unity Integration package has been installed and is ready for use.

To verify the plugin is enabled and ready, follow these steps:

1. Open the **Package Manager** window by clicking on **Window** from the **File** menu and then click on **Package Manager**:

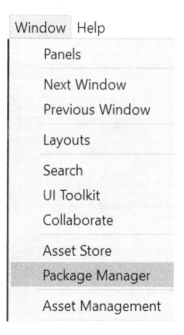

Figure 6.4 – Window menu with Package Manager selected in Unity

2. In the **Package Manager** window, click on the **Packages** drop-down menu and make sure **In Project** is selected:

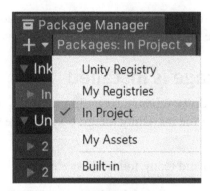

Figure 6.5 – Package Manager with the In Project option selected

3. The ink-Unity Integration plugin is ready for usage if it is included in a listing of packages currently in use with the project and has a green checkmark next to its name indicating it is installed in the current project.

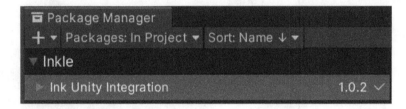

Figure 6.6 – Package manager showing the ink Unity Integration package installed

4. After verifying that the ink Unity Integration package is installed, the **Package Manager** window can be closed.

In the next section, we will move on to working with ink files. After installing the ink-Unity Integration Plugin, we will learn how to create ink files, edit them, and use the auto-compilation process built into the plugin.

Working with ink files

Unity is only aware of files inside of the folders it watches. To work with other files, they must be added as new assets to an existing project. With the ink-Unity Integration plugin installed, Unity will watch all new files with the `.ink` file type and will automatically compile them for usage in Unity projects based on its **Project Settings**. However, the first step is to add these Ink source files to an existing Unity project using the plugin.

Adding ink source files

Files created with Inky are saved with the .ink file type. These are *source* files for projects. They are the code form of Ink stories. To work with ink in Unity, the first step is to create a new .ink file.

To create a new ink source file in Unity, open an existing project and make sure the **Project** window is open. (If not open, it can be re-opened using the **Window** menu by clicking on **General** and then **Project**.)

There are often multiple ways of doing the same thing in Unity. This applies to creating new files in the **Project** window as well. One way to create new ink files is use the **Project** window's toolbar and the **Create** menu and then the **Ink** option. They can also be created by right-clicking in the **Project** window and going to the **Create** menu and then down to **Ink**:

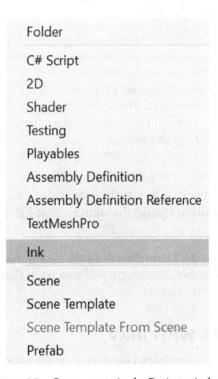

Figure 6.7 – Create menu in the Project window

The created Ink source file can either be renamed or the default name of New Ink can be accepted by clicking outside of its filename area. Moments after being created, the ink-Unity Integration plugin will generate a new file matching the name of the created one.

Figure 6.8 – ink-Unity Integration plugin generated file in Unity Project view

---

Auto-compilation setting

If Unity does not automatically generate a .json file based on the ink source file, the auto-compilation setting may be turned off. Consult the *Updating automatic re-compilation* section of the *Adjusting plugin settings* topic later in this chapter for how to change this setting.

Clicking on the generated file will reveal it is a .json file. When ink runs a story, it runs what it calls a **compiled project**. In ink, these are created by using the ink-Unity Integration plugin or other tools to change the source .ink file into a compiled .json file.

With the ink-Unity Integration plugin installed, a new .json file will automatically be created for every existing .ink file. The plugin will also track changes and re-compile the project every time it detects new changes.

Editing source files with Inky

ink source files are best edited using Inky. However, new ink source files are often added to a Unity project using its **Create** menu or moving a file into its folders. This can often make the file harder to find for editing in Inky. To fix this issue, new .ink files can be associated with Inky for editing when open within Unity.

Depending on the operating system, the instructions are different. The next two sections contain the steps for *Windows (10 and later)* and *macOS (11.1 and later)*.

Windows: Associating Inky with ink source files

To start to associate Inky with all .ink files in Windows 10 and later, follow these steps:

1. Click on a created file in the **Project** window of Unity. This will open it in the **Inspector** view:

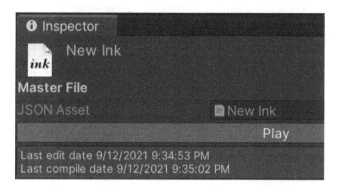

Figure 6.9 – Inspector view of an ink source file

2. Click on **Open** to open the file. This will prompt you for what program should be used to open this and future .ink files.

Figure 6.10 – File association prompt in Windows 10

3. Click on **More apps** and scroll to the bottom of the listing:

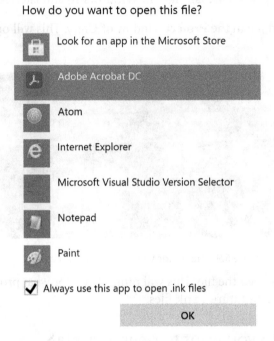

Figure 6.11 – Program listings in Windows 10

4. Click on **Look for another app on this PC**. This will open a prompt for the application to use. Navigate to where the Inky.exe file is found and select it:

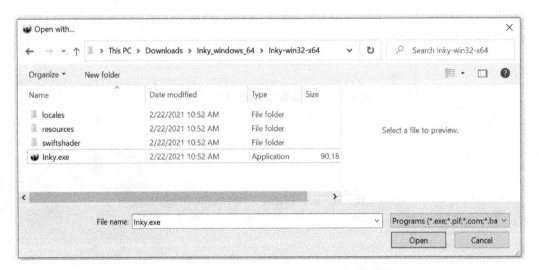

Figure 6.12 – Application chooser in Windows 10

5. Click **Open** to associate Inky with `.ink` files. After a few moments, Windows will then open the `.ink` file found in the **Project** window of Unity in Inky.

Moving forward, assuming the `Inky.exe` file is not deleted, Unity will redirect all file opening actions for `.ink` files to Inky.

macOS: Associating Inky with ink source files

To start to associate Inky with all `.ink` files in macOS (11.1 and later), follow these steps:

1. Right-click on a created file in the **Project** window of Unity. Click on **Reveal in Finder**:

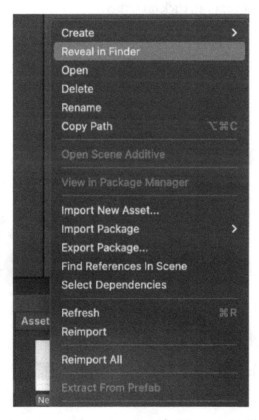

Figure 6.13 – File context menu for Unity in macOS

2. After Finder opens, right-click on the file and navigate to **Open With**:

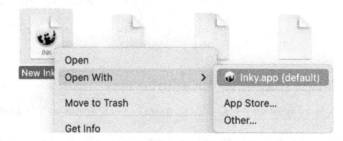

Figure 6.14 – Open With file context menu in macOS

3. If `Inky.app` does not appear, click on **Other…**:

Figure 6.15 – Application chooser in macOS

4. Search for `Inky` in the **Applications** folder and select `Inky.app` from the listing. Click on **Open**.

Moving forward, assuming the `Inky.app` file is not deleted, Unity will redirect all file opening actions for `.ink` files to Inky.

Updating ink source files

Once Inky has been associated with ink source files, editing the files becomes much easier. Double-clicking on the files in the **Project** window will open them in Inky. Because the Ink-Unity Integration plugin will automatically re-compile all changed Ink source files into `.json` files, this means both the source and compiled files will always be up to date.

1. To see this process in action, double-click on the created ink file from the `Adding Ink source files` section to open it in Inky.

2. Change its contents to the following `Example 1`:

   ```
   Hello! This is an Ink source file!
   ```

3. Save the file in Inky by clicking on **File** and then **Save Project**. Return to Unity.

   After detecting the file change, the ink-Unity Integration plugin will have re-compiled and generated a new `.json` file. The **Console** window will also show when this process started and was completed.

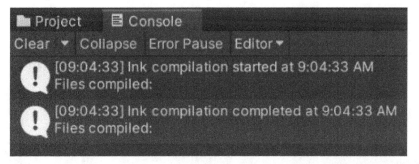

Figure 6.16 – Console window showing ink compilation messages

With Inky associated with `.ink` files and the ink-Unity Integration plugin installed in a Unity project, new Ink source files can be added to a Unity project and then edited with Inky. Every time they are saved, the ink-Unity Integration plugin will re-compile them based on its **Project Settings**. Updating ink source files becomes as easy as adding them to a Unity project and then editing them in Inky.

With the ink-Unity Integration plugin ready, we move ahead in the next section to examining its settings and how to update the auto-compilation functionality.

Adjusting plugin settings

The ink-Unity Integration plugin comes with multiple settings that can be changed depending on the needs of the Unity project. This topic will review how to find the **Project Settings** window and update a common option – automatic re-compilation.

Finding ink-Unity Integration settings

The Ink-Unity Integration plugin comes with default settings. These can be changed by editing them as part of **Project Settings**:

1. Click on Edit and then **Project Settings**:

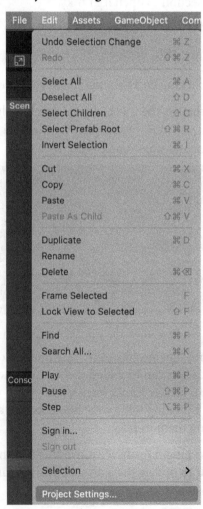

Figure 6.17 – Edit menu with Project Settings... selected

2. Click on **Ink** from the sidebar options to see the related settings for the project.

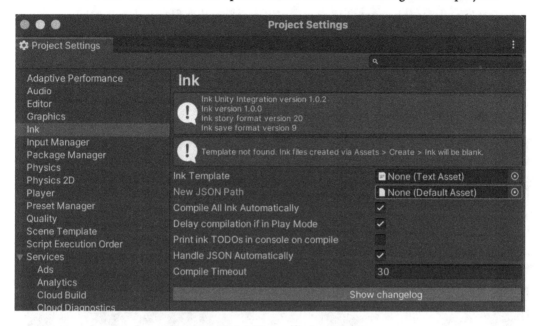

Figure 6.18 – Ink Project Settings in Unity

In the next section, we will use the **Project Settings** window to update a common setting, the automatic re-compilation of ink source files.

Updating automatic re-compilation

If a project has a large ink source file or many different smaller files each using the INCLUDE keyword in ink, the compilation process might take more than a few seconds each time files are changed. In these contexts, turning off the re-compilation of ink source files might prevent the ink-Unity Integration plugin from wasting time re-compiling the ink source files.

1. In the **Project Settings** window, click on **Ink**:

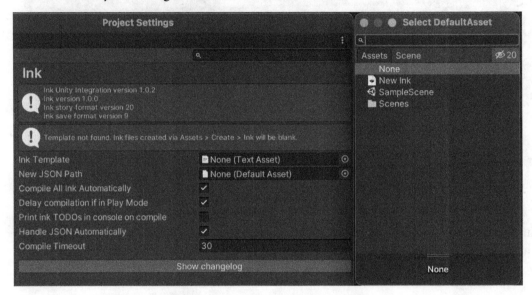

Figure 6.19 – Ink Project Settings in Unity

2. Click on the checkbox next to **Compile All Ink Automatically** to disable the automatic compilation process. (This can be re-enabled by clicking on the checkbox again later.)

In this topic, we examined the Ink **Project Settings** window and updated the auto-compilation option. Depending on the size of the ink source and other factors, the compilation process can sometimes take too long between changes. Updating the automatic compilation of ink sources files can often be a very useful setting to be aware of and update, depending on the project.

Summary

In this chapter, we learned how to find the ink-Unity Integration plugin online as part of the first topic. We reviewed how to import the package and then verify it was installed. This is an important step for all projects using the plugin, as it must be re-imported for any new project.

In the second topic, *Working with ink files*, we looked at how to create new ink files in Unity. We examined how to associate Inky with ink source files in both Windows 10 and macOS. We then learned how to edit ink files and how the ink-Unity Integration plugin will detect any changes and recreate the compiled JSON file if the option is enabled in the **Project Settings**.

Finally, in the *Adjusting plugin settings* topic, we looked at the settings when using the ink-Unity Integration plugin. We first reviewed how to find the **Project Settings** for the plugin by selecting **Ink** from the available options. Next, we examined how to adjust the automatic re-compilation of ink files.

In the next chapter, we'll move ahead to use the Ink API to work with a running story. The ink-Unity Integration plugin helps to generate the JSON files based on the ink source files. We will use the JSON files in the next chapter, and we will learn how to load parts of a story as part of a larger Unity project.

Questions

1. Does Inkle recommend using the Unity Asset Store?
2. What is at least one way to create an ink file using the ink-Unity Integration plugin in Unity?
3. What program is a good choice for editing ink files?
4. Can the auto-compilation process of the ink-Unity Integration plugin be changed?

7

Unity API – Making Choices and Story Progression

This chapter begins with reviewing how to add a `script` component to a game object in Unity. By creating a `script` component associated with a C# file, code can be written to load the compiled JSON files created by the ink-Unity Integration plugin from ink source files as part of the Unity scene. Next, we will examine how to load an ink story and start to progress through it. We will see how to programmatically make selections of options presented by ink and then how to continue story progression as a result. We will end with an example of a common approach of presenting multiple user interface elements to a player in Unity. A user will be able to click buttons in Unity and guide story progression in a running ink story.

In this chapter, we will cover the following main topics:

- Loading a compiled ink story
- Selecting options programmatically
- Creating a dynamic user interface

Technical requirements

The examples used in this chapter, in `*.ink` files, can be found online on GitHub: `https://github.com/PacktPublishing/Dynamic-Story-Scripting-with-the-ink-Scripting-Language/tree/main/Chapter7`.

Loading a compiled ink story

In *Chapter 6, Adding and Working with the ink-Unity Integration Plugin*, we saw how to add new ink files to a Unity project. After importing the plugin, new files can be created using the **Create** menu from the **Project** window. When an ink source was added, the plugin automatically created a compiled JSON file. As we now move into working with the ink API provided by the plugin, we will use the created JSON files for working with a story.

The first step for working with code in Unity is to create a `GameObject`. This is a basic container in Unity. Each `GameObject` holds at least one component. The different systems in Unity, such as the rendering system (for drawing things on a screen), physics (for detecting whether two things overlap on a screen), and input (for detecting whether a user presses a button) all communicate with these components. When Unity runs a project, it sends data to components matching the system associated with it. For example, to work with data from the input system, an input component is needed.

To work with code in Unity, a `script` component is needed. All code added to a Unity project works through being a part of different systems. A `script` component allows a developer to write code for working with a game object and the different components it contains. Unlike most other components that primarily receive data from different systems, a `script` component can *script* other objects and values. Through code, it can instruct other components to change their values when different events, such as a user clicking on a button, happen.

Creating a script component

Any game object can have a `script` component. However, for better organization, it is often useful to create a new `GameObject` for each type of data, behavior, or task related to a project. This separates each new action or possible event with a `GameObject` and makes working on the different parts of a larger project much easier:

1. Open a new or existing Unity project.
2. If not already added, be sure to install the ink-Unity Integration plugin.

There are always multiple ways to do things in Unity, and this is also true of creating a new game object. One of the easiest ways to create a new game object is by using the **GameObject** menu.

3. Click on **GameObject** and then click on **Create Empty**.

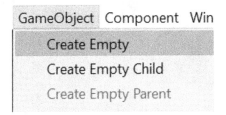

Figure 7.1 – GameObject menu

4. A new GameObject will be created and added to the **Hierarchy** view. Clicking on the created GameObject will show its current components in the **Inspector** view.

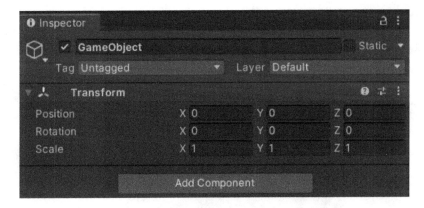

Figure 7.2 – Inspector view in Unity

Each GameObject is merely a container. Its components do all the work involved with running the project. Even the name of the GameObject is a value contained as part of its components.

5. To change the name of the created `GameObject`, click on it in the **Hierarchy** view to show its components in the **Inspector** view. Click on **text entry** and change the name from `GameObject` (the default value) to `Ink Story`.

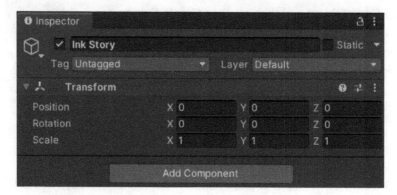

Figure 7.3 – Ink Story name change in Unity

The newly named `Ink Story` will be a container for other components related to running an ink story. Changing the name of the game object to `Ink Story` makes it easier to find it among potentially many other objects in the project and explains its role in the project as well.

6. With the components of `Ink Story` shown in the **Inspector** view, click on **Add Component**.

Figure 7.4 – Component listing in the Add Component menu

7. In the listing, click on **New script**.

Figure 7.5 – New script component creation

8. Name this new script file `inkLoader.cs`.

> **Note**
>
> Clicking on the `script` component name does not always allow access to rename the file in Unity. Pressing the down arrow twice on the keyboard will move the selection from the search to the title of the file.

Figure 7.6 – Script renamed InkLoader

9. After renaming the file, click the **Create and Add** button. A new C# file will be added to the **Project** window.

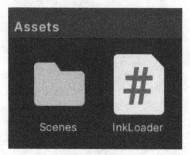

Figure 7.7 – Assets in Unity with the new InkLoader.cs file

10. Double-click on this file to open it in Visual Studio for editing.

This first section has included a step-by-step process of preparing a Unity project for working with the ink Story API. We have seen how to create a `GameObject` and add a `script` component. In the next section, we will build on this project to begin to work with the Story API added to Unity as part of the ink-Unity Integration plugin.

Adding the ink Story API

Installing the ink-Unity Integration plugin adds an additional **namespace** for use with C# code in Unity. A namespace is a collection of classes and methods collected under a common name and set of actions. The namespace added by the ink-Unity Integration plugin is called `Ink`. It contains, in turn, three other namespaces named `Parsed`, `Runtime`, and `UnityIntegration`, each of which contains classes related to their names. To work with compiled ink JSON files, the `Ink.Runtime` namespace is needed. This tells Unity that it should start with the `ink` namespace and then find the namespace within it named `Runtime`:

1. In the file opened in the *Creating a script component* section, add a new `using` line after those already there in the created file:

```
using System.Collections;
using System.Collections.Generic;
using UnityEngine;
using Ink.Runtime;
```

The `using` keyword tells Unity to include the `Ink.Runtime` namespace and allow its classes to be used as part of this file.

2. Next, create a public field called `inkJSONAsset` and change the `Start()` method to the following:

```
public class InkLoader: MonoBehaviour
{
    public TextAsset InkJSONAsset;

    // Start is called before the first frame update
    void Start()
    {
        Story exampleStory = new Story
        (InkJSONAsset.text);
    }
}
```

The use of the `InkJSONAsset` field with the `public` keyword will allow this value to be changed inside the Unity editor. The addition of the `Story` class creates a new ink story as part of the `Runtime` namespace. This is known as the *Story API* because multiple methods will be used as part of the `Story` class.

3. Save the `InkLoader.cs` file in Visual Studio and return to Unity.

4. After a moment, Unity will refresh and reload the changed C# file.

5. The final step is to associate an ink JSON file with the created C# file. In the **Hierarchy** view, click on the `InkStory` game object. In the **Inspector** view, there will be a new property under the `script` component, as shown in the following screenshot:

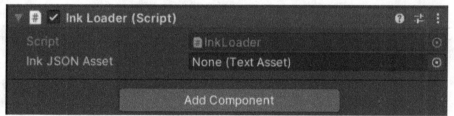

Figure 7.8 – New Ink JSON Asset property in the Inspector view

The property shows the value `None (Text Asset)`. This means no files are associated with this property. To change this, a compiled JSON file needs to be added.

> **Note**
>
> An ink JSON file will be needed for the next steps. If one is not created, add a new one by creating an ink file and letting the **Automatic compile** option create one, or click on an existing ink source file and then click on **Compile** in the **Inspector** view to create a new JSON file.

6. Click on the **TextAsset** selection circle next to the value to open a **Select TextAsset** window.

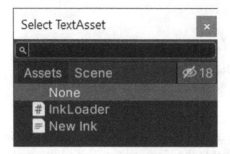

Figure 7.9 – Select TextAsset window

7. Select an ink-compiled JSON file.

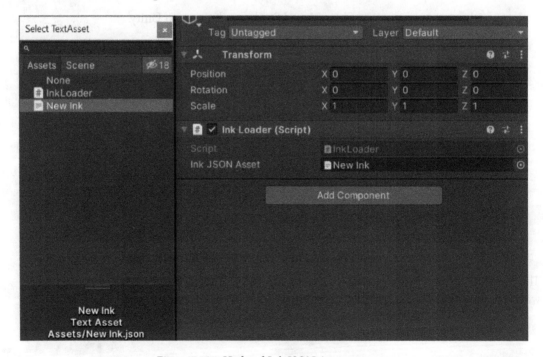

Figure 7.10 – Updated Ink JSON Asset property

After the value of the **Ink JSON Asset** property updates, close the **Select TextAsset** window.

8. Click on the **Play** button in the middle of the Unity editor.

Figure 7.11 – Play button in Unity

Unity will run the current scene, and nothing will appear to happen. If no errors appear in the **Console** window, everything has run correctly. Internally, Unity has loaded the compiled ink JSON file and is ready to run the ink story.

Stop the running scene by clicking on the **Play** button a second time.

Running an ink JSON file

ink stories are run using the `Story` class and methods. Loading an ink JSON file is only the first step. The `Story` class must be told to load one or more *lines* of the story at a time.

When Inky was used to run the ink source file previously, it displayed one line at a time with an empty line between them:

Example 1:

```
This is the start.
And then this happens.
```

When run in Inky, *Example 1* creates the following output:

This is the start.

And then this happens.

End of story

Figure 7.12 – Example 1 output

In Inky, the extra lines it created are a result of its own use of the Story API. To replicate this output, we will need to add a new method: `Continue()`:

1. In the same file used as part of the *Adding the ink Story API* section, open the file in Inky for editing.

2. Change the content of the new ink source file to *Example 1* and then save the file in Inky. Do not close Inky after saving the file. Now return to Unity.

3. Upon detecting the change in the ink source file, the ink-Unity Integration plugin will automatically re-compile the ink JSON file. Because it was associated with the Ink JSON Asset property as part of the *Adding the ink Story API* section, the ink JSON file will also always be loaded correctly.

4. If the `InkLoader.cs` file is not already open in Visual Studio, double-click on it in the **Project** window.

5. Add the following line to the `Start()` method:

```
void Start()
{
Story exampleStory = new Story(InkJSONAsset.text);
    Debug.Log(exampleStory.Continue());
}
```

6. Save the changed `inkLoader.cs` file and return to Unity.

7. Click on the **Play** button to run the current scene.

    This time, the **Console** window will show a message.

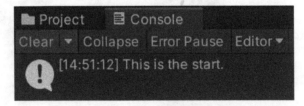

Figure 7.13 – Console window in Unity

The `Debug.Log()` method used what was returned by the `Continue()` method as part of the `Story` class to display a message in the **Console** window.

Each time the `Continue()` method is called, it loads the next line in an ink story and returns a string representing it. However, the method has an issue: it cannot detect the end of a story. For that, a different property is required.

Stop the running scene by clicking on the **Play** button again.

Checking whether a story can continue

The Continue() method loads the next line of a story if it is available. In the code from *Example 1*, there are two lines.

1. Return to Visual Studio and edit the InkLoader.cs file. Change the Story() method to the following:

```
void Start()
{
Story exampleStory = new Story(InkJSONAsset.text);
Debug.Log(exampleStory.Continue());
Debug.Log(exampleStory.Continue());
}
```

2. Save the InkLoader.cs file after adding the new line of code. Return to Unity and click on the **Play** button to play the current scene and updated file.

3. The **Console** window will show two messages.

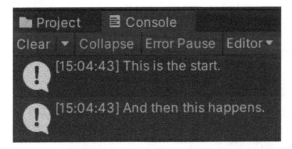

Figure 7.14 – Example 1 content loaded via the Continue() method

Both lines from *Example 1* are now shown in the **Console** window. Each one was loaded by the Continue() method and then passed to the Debug.Log() method.

4. Click on the **Play** button again in Unity to stop the current scene.

5. Return to Visual Studio and edit the InkLoader.cs file. Add the following code to the Start() method:

```
void Start()
{
Story exampleStory = new Story(InkJSONAsset.text);
Debug.Log(exampleStory.Continue());
Debug.Log(exampleStory.Continue());
```

```
Debug.Log(exampleStory.Continue());
}
```

6. Save the updated `InkLoader.cs` file.

7. Return to Unity and play the scene.

    With the third use of the `Continue()` method, an error will happen and be displayed in the **Console** window.

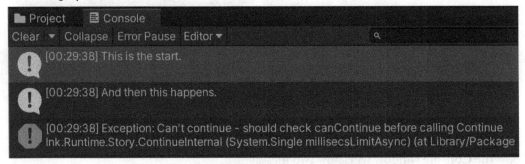

Figure 7.15 – Continue() error in the Unity console

8. Click on the **Play** button in Unity to stop the scene from running.

    The error happened because the `Continue()` method does not check whether there is another line to load. When there is no more content, it throws an error.

    To fix this issue, a property mentioned in the error is needed. The `Story` class provides the `canContinue` property for checking whether there is more story content to load. It contains a Boolean value. If there is more content, `canContinue` will be `true`. Otherwise, it will be `false`.

9. Return to Visual Studio and edit the `InkLoader.cs` file. Update the `Start()` method in the `InkLoader.cs` file to the following:

```
void Start()
{
Story exampleStory = new Story(InkJSONAsset.text);

while(exampleStory.canContinue)
    {
        Debug.Log(exampleStory.Continue());
    }
}
```

10. Save the edited `InkLoader.cs` file in Visual Studio.

11. Return to Unity and play the scene again.

With the use of a `while` loop, the story will be loaded line by line until there is no content left. Once this happens, the `canContinue` property is changed to `false` and the loop ends.

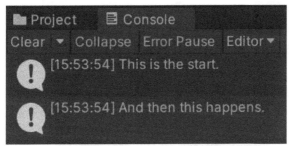

Figure 7.16 – Console window using an updated while loop

The combination of the `canContinue` property with the `Continue()` method is a common pattern when using the Story API. More advanced usage patterns may not use a `while` loop, but the property and method will often appear together.

Selecting options programmatically

Displaying only the text of an ink story has limited usefulness. Most advanced ink stories use weaves to present different options. Along with the `Continue()` method and the `canContinue` property, the Story API also has another property called `currentChoices` that contains a list of the options generated by the most recent weave.

As was demonstrated in the *Checking whether a story can continue* section, the `canContinue` property is affected by the `Continue()` method. After each line is loaded and returned as a string, the `Story` class will update the `canContinue` property if there is more story to load. This is also true of the `currentChoice` property. When the `Continue()` method is used, it will load the next line *and* any weaves.

Note

Any previously used game objects or C# files created as part of this chapter can safely be deleted. This section will create a new game object and script component, and use different code for working with weaves and options.

Detecting ink choices

The first step to act on a weave is to detect that its choices have been loaded by the currentChoices property. This means both the canContinue property and Continue() method are also needed. The first prevents any issues of trying to load content that may not exist and the second loads the current line and any weaves along the way:

1. In a new or existing Unity project with no other game objects using the Story API, create a new, empty GameObject. Name it Ink Choices.

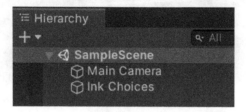

Figure 7.17 – ink Choices GameObject

2. As was shown in the *Creating a script component* section, create a new script component on the Ink Choices game object. Name this new file LoadingChoices.cs.

Figure 7.18 – LoadingChoices.cs file in the Assets window

3. Double-click on the `LoadingChoices.cs` file in the **Assets** window to open it for editing in Visual Studio:

```
using System.Collections;
using System.Collections.Generic;
using UnityEngine;
using Ink.Runtime;


public class LoadingChoices : MonoBehaviour
{
    public TextAsset InkJSONAsset;

    void Start()
    {
        Story InkStory = new Story(InkJSONAsset.text);
        InkStory.Continue();
        foreach (Choice c in InkStory.currentChoices)
        {
            Debug.Log(c.text);
        }
    }
}
```

4. Save the file in Visual Studio and return to Unity.

5. Create a new ink file and name (or rename) the file to `Example3.ink`.

Figure 7.19 – Example3.ink file in the Assets window

6. Following the instructions in the *Running an ink JSON file* section, associate the automatically generated ink JSON file with the `Ink Choices` game object property.

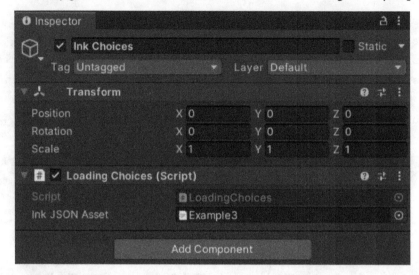

Figure 7.20 – Example3.json file associated with the ink JSON Asset property

7. Open the `Example3.ink` file for editing in Inky. Change it to the following:

```
Sam reached out, not quite touching Juan.


* "Are you just going to leave me?"
* "He didn't mean anything to me!"
* "Can't we just start again?"
```

8. Save the changed `Example3.ink` file. Return to Unity and run the scene. The **Console** window in Unity will now show the text content of each option.

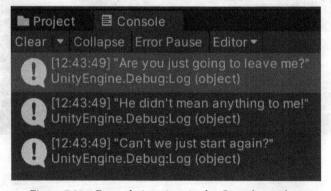

Figure 7.21 – Example 3 options in the Console window

The use of the Continue() method loaded not only the first line of *Example 3* but also the first weave appearing within the code. The currentChoices property contains a List<Choice> of objects per choice that exists within the weave. Each element of List<Choice> is a Choice object, a special class containing two important properties: index and text.

Within the foreach loop, the text property of each Choice object is retrieved. This is then passed to the Debug.Log() method. When run, the ink story is loaded. Next, the first line and weave are loaded. Inside the loop, the currentChoices property is used to retrieve the value of each text property. Each is then shown in the **Console** window using the Debug.Log() method.

Making choices using the Unity API

Options are selected by players to continue a story. Within the ink source code, a choice is created using either the asterisk (*) or the plus symbol (+). When run, the ink runtime code as part of the Story class creates *options* from these source code choices. However, to progress in an ink story, a choice must be *made*. It must exist in the code and then be presented as an option.

The Story class provides a method named ChooseChoiceIndex(). This accepts an *index* (int) within the range of the current total number of elements in the currentChoices property. Each Choice object within the list of currentChoices has index and text properties. In the *Detecting ink choices* section, the text property was used to display the generated option from the ink source file. To *make* a choice, its index property is used:

1. Double-click on the LoadingChoices.cs file from the *Detecting ink choices* section to open it for editing if it is not already open in Visual Studio.

2. Update the file to the following:

```
void Start()
{
Story InkStory = new Story(InkJSONAsset.text);
InkStory.Continue();
Choice exampleChoice = InkStory.currentChoices[0];
InkStory.ChooseChoiceIndex(exampleChoice.index);
Debug.Log(InkStory.Continue());
}
```

3. Save the file in Visual Studio, return to Unity, and run the scene.

The **Console** window will show the text of the choice matching the first (0) position element within the `currentChoices` property.

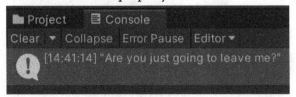

Figure 7.22 – Option chosen from Example 3 in the Console window

The `ChooseChoiceIndex()` method selects the first choice within the weave based on the `index` property of `exampleChoice`. This is then displayed in the Unity **Console** window using the `Continue()` method.

To *make* choices when using ink and Unity, a combination of things needs to happen in sequence. First, a story must be loaded. Second, at least one line needs to be loaded that also contains a weave. Next, the `currentChoices` property of the `Story` class must be used to retrieve the created options for the player. The `ChooseChoiceIndex()` method then needs to be used with the `index` property of one of the `Choice` objects retrieved from the `currentChoices` property. Finally, the next part of the story needs to be loaded. This additional loading will include the text of the option (if selective output is not used) chosen using the `ChooseChoiceIndex()` method. The rest of the story can then proceed.

Loading all text until the next weave

While useful for loading story content, the `Continue()` method must be used multiple times to load each line at a time. As with the code in the *Making choices using the Unity API* section, this means it would need to appear across multiple lines of code. Anticipating this problem, the Story API also includes a method named `ContinueMaximally()`.

Instead of loading a line at a time, the `ContinueMaximally()` method loads all content until it encounters a weave. For many projects, this is a preferred method to use when there might be multiple lines of text between weaves or generated by ink internally as a part of the weave itself:

1. Create a new ink source file in Unity. Name (or rename) the file to `Example4.ink`.

2. Open `Example4.ink` for editing in Inky and update it to the following:

```
You read all the books and convinced your parents into
going to the zoo. You just had to know.

You enter the area containing the snakes and walk up to
the glass.
```

```
-> snake_house

== snake_house

+ (tap){tap < 2}[Tap the glass and say something {tap >
0: again}]
    {tap <= 1: You tap on the glass in front of you.
      The snake turns slightly toward the noise and
      sticks out its tongue.}
    {tap > 1: No, you finally decide. You cannot talk
      to snakes.}
    -> snake_house
+ [Ignore the snake]
    You regard the coiled snake and then walk out.
    {tap > 1: What were you thinking? Talking to
      snakes is fictional.}
    -> DONE
```

3. Update the Example4.ink file with the content from *Example 4*.

4. Click on the **Ink Choices** game object and then, in the **Inspector** view, change the associated file from Example3.json to Example4.json.

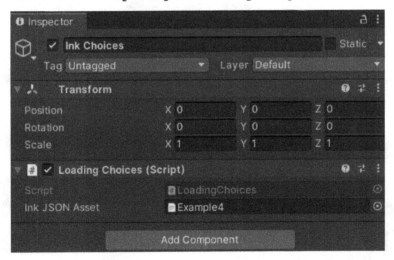

Figure 7.23 – Updated Example4.json value in the Inspector view

5. Double-click on LoadingChoices.cs to open it for editing in Visual Studio.

6.   Update the file to the following:

```
using System.Collections;
using System.Collections.Generic;
using UnityEngine;
using Ink.Runtime;


public class LoadingChoices : MonoBehaviour
{
    public TextAsset InkJSONAsset;


    void Start()
    {
        Story InkStory = new Story(InkJSONAsset.text);
        Debug.Log(InkStory.ContinueMaximally());
        Choice exampleChoice =
        InkStory.currentChoices[0];
        Debug.Log(exampleChoice.text);
        InkStory.ChooseChoiceIndex
           (exampleChoice.index);
        Debug.Log(InkStory.ContinueMaximally());
    }
}
```

7.   Save the changes in Visual Studio, return to Unity, and run the scene.

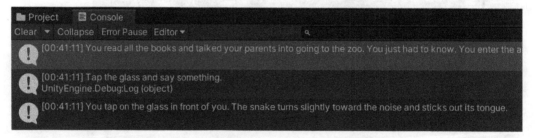

Figure 7.24 – Loaded lines and choice text from Example 4

8.   Stop the running scene.

The first usage of the `ContinueMaximally()` method loaded the first two lines and the weave. Next, the `ChooseChoiceIndex()` method chose the first option. The second `ContinueMaximally()` method usage, when paired with the internal divert, then loaded the next line and the weave again.

When working with looping structures, the `ContinueMaximally()` method is often better than using the `Continue()` method. Use of the `ContinueMaximally()` method will always load all the new text until it encounters the next weave. For loops where text might appear between weaves, a single use of the `ContinueMaximally()` method would achieve the same effect as multiple calls to the `Continue()` method to load the same content.

This topic started with detecting choices in a running ink story with the `currentChoices` property. We then moved into making choices, both creating them in the ink code and then using the `ChooseChoiceIndex()` method to pick them. Finally, we saw how the `ContinueMaximally()` method can be combined with both the `currentChoices` property and the `ChooseChoiceIndex()` method. In the next topic, we will expand on these concepts. To create a dynamic interface, we can use our knowledge of the Story API to associate the `GameObjects` user interface and create a connection between clicking a button on the screen and progressing an ink story.

Creating a dynamic user interface

The `Story` class provides multiple methods for loading and progressing a story. However, without a user interface, a player is not able to select between options and see the result. To fix this problem, additional game objects are needed to show text and provide an interface for a user to click on different things.

To start, a new project is needed. Instead of example code, this will use different user interface objects for working with a user. The project will also need to create a **Prefab**. In Unity, a `GameObject` can become *prefabricated* by moving it from the **Hierarchy** view into the **Project** window. This allows its settings and values to be kept as an asset in the project. Prefabs in Unity can also be **instantiated**, a process by which C# code can create a copy of an existing `GameObject` during runtime.

The current lines as returned by the `ContinueMaximally()` method and choices in the `currentChoices` property can potentially be dynamic while an ink story runs. Combined with a Prefab, C# code can recreate an interface dynamically because of a player clicking on buttons to make choices in a story.

In this topic, we will move through the steps of creating a dynamic interface by starting with a new Unity project and creating the necessary game objects. Next, we will associate a Prefab with our code. Finally, we will end with a section on putting everything together and running the combined project.

Creating a new project and game objects

Let us now start with creating a new project and game objects:

1. Create a new project in Unity. Name this project The Body and use a 2D template.

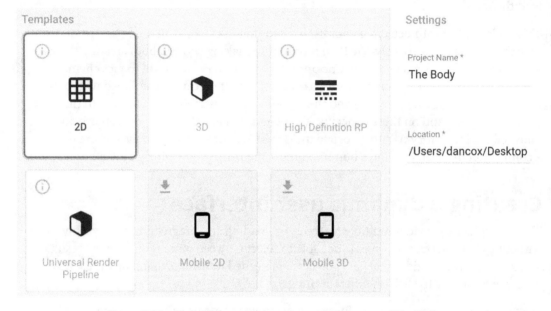

Figure 7.25 – Unity Hub project creation with the name of The Body

> **Important Note**
> Before doing anything else, install the ink-Unity Integration plugin in the new project using the instructions as part of *Chapter 6, Adding and Working with the ink-Unity Integration Plugin*.

2. Once the project has been created by Unity, add a Canvas game object to the **Hierarchy** view.

A new `Canvas` game object can be accessed by selecting **UI** and then **Canvas** from the **GameObject** menu.

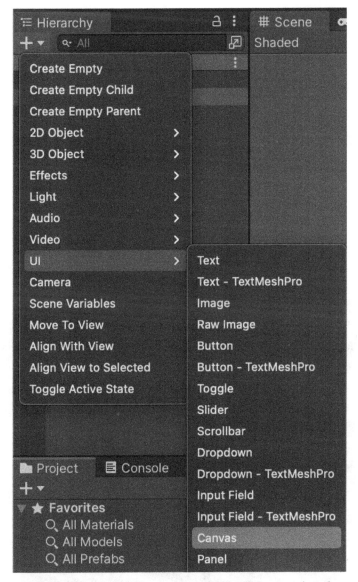

Figure 7.26 – GameObject menu with UI and Canvas selected

By adding a `Canvas` game object, Unity will automatically add an `EventSystem` game object.

3. Click on the `Canvas` game object. In the **Inspector** view, click on the **Add Component** button. Select **Layout** and then **Vertical Layout Group**.

Figure 7.27 – Vertical Layout Group component selection

A vertical layout group will automatically align all other UI game objects within itself in a *vertical* pattern.

4. In the vertical layout group, click on the **Child Alignment** dropdown and select **Middle Center**.

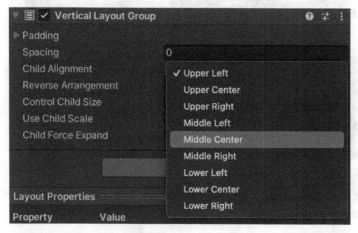

Figure 7.28 – Vertical Layout Group with Middle Center selected

5. With the Canvas game object selected in the **Hierarchy** view, create a new Text game object. Text game objects can be found under **UI** and then **Text**. The created Text will be added as a child of the Canvas game object.

Figure 7.29 – Added Text game object in the Hierarchy view

6. With the Canvas game object selected in the **Hierarchy** view, create a Button game object. Button can be found under **UI** and then **Button**. The created Button game object will be added as a child of the Canvas game object.

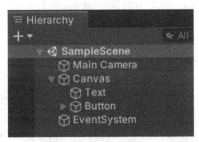

Figure 7.30 – Added Button game object in the Hierarchy view

7. Select the newly added Button game object, and then click and drag it from the **Hierarchy** view to the **Project** window. This will create a Prefab based on the Button in the **Project** window.

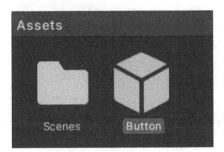

Figure 7.31 – Prefab created in the Project window

8. After the `Button` game object icon changes in the **Hierarchy** view, delete the `Button` game object in the **Hierarchy** view only. Because the `Button` game object is now a Prefab, it exists as an asset and does not need to exist in the current **Hierarchy** view. (It will later be instantiated by code.)

With the project and game objects created, the next item is a `script` component. This will create the necessary properties for other files to be associated with running the story.

Associating Prefab and ink JSON files

After creating the game objects in the last section, we will now create a `script` component, create the necessary properties, and then associate assets with the properties:

1. Select the `Canvas` game object in the **Hierarchy** view.

2. In the **Inspector** view, create a new `script` component using the instructions in the *Creating a script component* section.

3. Name (or rename following creation) this new file `InkStory.cs`.

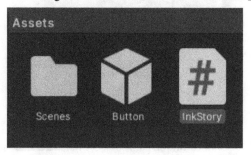

Figure 7.32 – Created InkStory.cs file

4. Double-click on the `InkStory.cs` file for editing in Visual Studio.

5. Update the code to the following:

```
using System.Collections;
using System.Collections.Generic;
using UnityEngine;
using Ink.Runtime;

public class InkStory : MonoBehaviour
{
    public TextAsset InkJSONAsset;
    public GameObject prefabButton;
}
```

There are three new additions to the default code provided by Unity. The first is the inclusion of the Ink.Runtime namespace. This will allow us to work with ink while a story runs. The second two additions are the properties we will be using in the **Inspector** view in the Unity editor. To associate assets with code, we can use the public keyword in C# to create a property we can adjust in the editor:

1. Save the file and return to Unity.

2. Create a new ink file named (or renamed following creation) TheBody.ink.

3. Open the TheBody.ink file in Inky for editing and copy the contents from the file from GitHub.

> **Note**
>
> The code for this example, TheBody.ink, can be found on GitHub.

4. Save the ink source file and return to Unity.

   The use of the public keyword in InkStory.cs added two new properties to the Canvas game object.

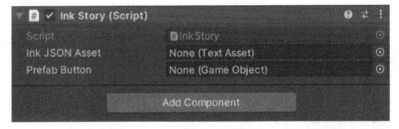

Figure 7.33 – Properties added in the Inspector view

5. Click on the file selection next to the Ink JSON Asset property to open the **Select TextAsset** window.

6. Associate the ink JSON file created by the ink-Unity Integration plugin with the **Ink JSON Asset** property and then close the **Select TextAsset** window.

7. Click on the file selection next to the Button Prefab to open the **Select GameObject** window.

8. Select the **Assets** tab in the **Select GameObject** window if it is not open.

9. Select the **Button** Prefab and then close the **Select GameObject** window.

The result of associating the ink JSON file with the `Button` Prefab will be that the code has access to those assets during runtime.

Figure 7.34 – Updated Ink Story component with the ink JSON file and button Prefab values

With the file associated with properties of the `script` component, additional code can now be written. Changing the ink source file, `TheBody.ink`, and saving the change will automatically update the `TheBody.json` file. The same is also true of the `Button` Prefab. It can also be adjusted, and its settings changed. As long as neither asset is renamed, Unity will maintain the association and allow developers to customize their settings independent of the code using them when the scene runs.

By the end of this section, we will have created a Unity project, its game objects, and associated assets with properties. Before we can run the project, we will need to write more code to dynamically create a user interface based on the content of a running ink story. In the next section, we will write the code to use the Prefab and create a dynamic interface based on the text output of the `ContinueMaximally()` method and the `currentChoices` property.

Making a dynamic user interface

The final series of steps needed before the Unity project can be run is to add more code. We need to incorporate the concepts explained in this chapter covering the use of the `ContinueMaximally()` method and the `currentChoices` property. We also need to add an overall loop within the code using the `canContinue` property to check whether there is more content before progressing the story.

We begin by adding the properties we will need within the class that will not be used by the Unity editor. We mark these using the `private` keyword.

Open `InkStory.cs` for editing in Visual Studio:

```
using System.Collections;
using System.Collections.Generic;
using UnityEngine;
using UnityEngine.UI;
```

```
using Ink.Runtime;


public class InkStory : MonoBehaviour
{
    public TextAsset InkJSONAsset;
    public GameObject prefabButton;

    private Story inkStory;
    private Text currentLinesText;
}
```

To work with user interface game objects, another instance of the using keyword is needed. This adds access to classes such as Text and Button used in this file.

The Story class and the Text game object currentLinesText will be used across methods in this code. To make sure they can be used in this way, they must be properties of the InkStory class and not variables within any method.

The first thing that must happen is the loading of the ink JSON file. Next, a reference to the Text component is needed. The text will be shown to the user each time they make a choice. This means the text property of the Text game object will need to be updated. However, as it is a child of Canvas, the GetComponentInChildren() method is needed:

```
void Start()
{
inkStory = new Story(InkJSONAsset.text);
currentLinesText = GetComponentInChildren<Text>();
}
```

The process of loading the text content and current choices will be used multiple times. This means all the code used as part of the process should be its own method:

```
void LoadTextAndWeave()
{
if (inkStory.canContinue)
{
currentLinesText.text = inkStory.ContinueMaximally();

foreach (Choice c in inkStory.currentChoices)
```

```
{
GameObject cloneButtonGameObject =
  Instantiate(prefabButton, this.transform);

Button cloneButtonButton =
  cloneButtonGameObject.GetComponent<Button>();
cloneButtonButton.onClick.AddListener(delegate
{
inkStory.ChooseChoiceIndex(c.index);
LoadTextAndWeave();
                  });

Text cloneButtonText = cloneButtonButton.
  GetComponentInChildren<Text>();
cloneButtonText.text = c.text;
}
}
}
```

In the new `LoadTextAndWeave()` method, new text content will be loaded if the `canContinue` property is true. Using the `foreach` keyword, new buttons will be added by using the `Instantiate()` method in Unity. This *instantiates* a Prefab as a GameObject during runtime, creating it through code and adding it to the running scene.

Finally, the `AddListener()` method is used with the `OnClick` property of a button in Unity. This adds to a collection of which functions should be notified that a click has happened. The `delegate` keyword allows a developer to pass a method as an argument to another method. In this case, a short method is created within the same scope as the `foreach` loop. The `index` property can thus be used inside this created method.

Every time the button is clicked, the `Story` class method `ChooseChoiceIndex()` will be called with the correct index, and the `LoadTextAndWeave()` method will be called again, refreshing the value of the `currentLinesText` method and updating the current buttons shown on the screen:

1. To run the current code, one more change is needed. The `LoadTextAndWeave()` method needs to be called inside the `Start()` method:

    ```
    void Start()
    {
    ```

```
inkStory = new Story(InkJSONAsset.text);
currentLinesText = GetComponentInChildren<Text>();
LoadTextAndWeave();
}
```

2. Save the current code in Visual Studio. Return to Unity and run the scene.

    Immediately, two problems will become evident. First, the default black text on a dark background makes the text impossible to read. Second, only the first few words will be shown.

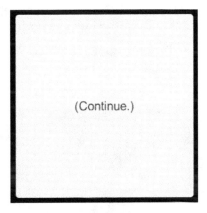

Figure 7.35 – The Body project running in Unity

3. Click on the **(Continue.)** button to see two more problems.

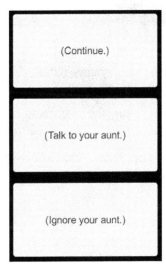

Figure 7.36 – Dynamically created buttons in The Body

The first problem is that instead of replacing the first button, Unity added two more. This is caused by the second call to the LoadTextAndWeave() method internally. First, the text content and button were loaded. Next, when the **(Continue.)** button was clicked, it was called again, adding more buttons.

We can also observe that the buttons are small and hard to read. By default, Unity will assume some values for a Button game object. While adjusting our code, we will also need to change the properties:

1. Stop the running scene.

2. To start to fix the issue with the text, first, select the Text game object in the **Hierarchy** view. The default values of its width and height are 160 and 30.

3. Through either clicking and dragging using the **Rect Transform** tool, or by changing the number directly, update their values to a width of 800 and height of 300.

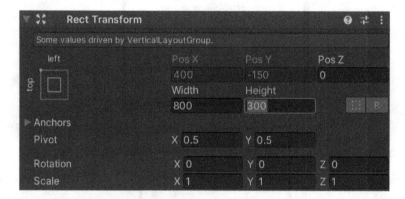

Figure 7.37 – The Inspector view in Unity with updated width and height values

4. Click on the **Font Size** property and change its value from 14 to 24. This will make the starting size larger.

5. Click on the **Color** property. Change the color from its default to white and then close the **Color** window.

    The updated values will now display more text and, with the white on a darker background, increase its readability.

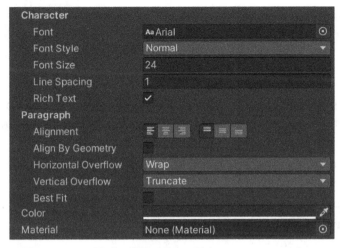

Figure 7.38 – Updated Text GameObject component values

6. Click on the Button Prefab in the **Project** window.

7. Like the Text game object, its default width is 160 and its height is 30. Change the width to 250 and the height to 100.

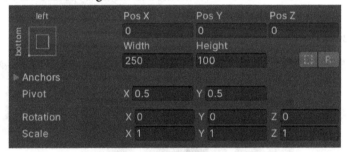

Figure 7.39 – Updated button Prefab values

8. Return to editing InkStory.cs in Visual Studio.

The fix to the code is a small but important one. Each time the button is clicked, the code will need to destroy the current buttons and then create new ones:

1. A new method is needed for the specific task of destroying Button children:

```
void DestroyButtonChildren()
{
    foreach (Transform child in transform)
    {
        if(child.tag == "ButtonChoice")
        {
```

```
        GameObject.Destroy(child.gameObject);
    }
  }
}
```

The new `DestroyButtonChildren()` method needs to be called as part of the delegate method. Before the content is refreshed, the current buttons need to be destroyed:

```
cloneButtonButton.onClick.AddListener(delegate
{
inkStory.ChooseChoiceIndex(c.index);
DestoryButtonChildren();
LoadTextAndWeave();
});
```

2. Save the updated file in Visual Studio and return to Unity.

The `DestroyButtonChildren()` method looks for a specific `tag` value. This needs to be added to the `Button` Prefab.

3. Select the `Button` Prefab in the **Project** window.

4. In the **Inspector** view, click on the **Tag** drop-down menu and then the **Add Tag...** option.

Figure 7.40 – Tag drop-down menu in the Unity Inspector view

5. Click on the + icon to add a new tag to the list. In the prompt, use the name *ButtonChoice.*

Figure 7.41 – New tag name

6. Click on **Save** to create a new tag.

7. Click on the Button Prefab in the **Project** window to open its values in the **Inspector** view.

Now that the ButtonChoice tag has been added, it must be selected.

8. In the **Tag** dropdown, select **ButtonChoice**.

Figure 7.42 – Added ButtonChoice option to the Tag drop-down menu

9. Run the scene. Play through the story by clicking on buttons to make choices and see the result.

10. Stop the running scene when done playing the story.

The changes to the Text game object and code will load the new text and correctly update the choices as the player clicks on the buttons. While consisting of multiple steps, this same approach can be used with most ink JSON files to present text and dynamic buttons for a player to make different choices and then see the result on the screen.

Summary

In this chapter, we worked through the process of adding a `script` component, associating an ink JSON file with a property, and using methods and properties as part of the `Story` class to progress a running ink story. We saw how the `Continue()` method loads one line at a time and the `ContinueMaximally()` method loads all text until it encounters a weave. When combined with the `canContinue` property, these methods allow for text content to be loaded from an ink JSON file and prevent any errors when the content runs out. With the `currentChoices` property, we examined how to use loops, such as those using the `foreach` keyword. When we used the `ChooseChoiceIndex()` method, we picked which option among the weave we wanted and progressed through a story using the `Continue()` or `ContinueMaximally()` methods again.

By setting up user interface game objects in Unity, we built a dynamic process to load ink story content, destroy buttons, and then create new ones. Needing to create a `Button` Prefab, we saw how these could be instantiated by the code while it was running. Adjusting the values of `Text` and `Button` game objects, we completed an interface for running an ink JSON file and built a system usable by many other projects working with the same game objects and organization.

In the next chapter, we continue to use the `Story` class and its methods. We will examine how to retrieve and update the values of variables in an ink story using C# code. We will also see ways of accessing functions in ink and how to pass data in and out of them. Combined with user interface game objects, we will build an example of how to communicate between the ink runtime and Unity code by using content from ink to create multiple dynamic interfaces in Unity.

Questions

1. What is the difference between the `Continue()` and `ContinueMaximally()` methods in the `Story` class?

2. What type of data does the `ChooseChoiceIndex()` method in the `Story` class expect?

3. How is the `canContinue` property used with the `Continue()` and `ContinueMaximally()` methods in the `Story` class?

4. What is a Prefab in Unity?

5. What type of object is found in the `currentChoices` list property of the `Story` class?

8

Story API – Accessing ink Variables and Functions

In this chapter, we will discuss how to use the ink Unity API to work with variables and functions. Any variables or functions defined in ink can be accessed from any point in its code. The API provided by the ink-Unity Integration plugin provides an interface through its `variablesState` property to access any defined variables. This is also true of a method provided by the `EvaluateFunction()` API, which can access any functions defined in the ink code. Understanding this functionality is key to creating more complex projects by using the ink-Unity Integration plugin as a bridge between an ink story and Unity code.

In this chapter, we will cover the following main topics:

- Changing ink variables outside a story
- Calling ink functions externally
- Controlling a story through variables and functions

Technical requirements

The examples used in this chapter, in the *.cs and *.ink files, can be found on GitHub at https://github.com/PacktPublishing/Dynamic-Story-Scripting-with-the-ink-Scripting-Language/tree/main/Chapter8.

Changing ink variables outside a story

Variables were first introduced in *Chapter 4, Variables, Lists, and Functions*. In ink, variables are created using the VAR keyword and an initial value. Throughout a story, the value of a variable can be changed. By comparing their values, variables can also influence the flow of a story.

Variables are *global* in ink. Once created, they can be accessed by any other part of the code within the same story. This functionality is also carried over into a named property as part of the ink-Unity Integration plugin, called variablesState. Every variable defined in an Ink story can be accessed by using its name.

In this topic, we will examine how to use this property to access and change values in a running ink story. We will begin by looking at how to use the variablesState property and comparing values in ink to control its flow outside the story.

Accessing ink variables

The Story API in Unity provides access to ink variables. In this section, we will explore the variablesState property and how to access an ink variable by its name. Perform the following steps:

1. Start by creating a new project in Unity based on the 2D built-in template.

2. Import the ink-Unity Integration plugin.

3. Add a new ink file and rename it InkVariables.ink.

   The file that is created will hold the ink source code. Because the ink-Unity Integration plugin runs compiled ink stories, the source code for a story must exist before the API can be used to access and run its contents:

Figure 8.1 – The project window showing the InkVariables.ink file

4. Open the `InkVariables.ink` file for editing in Inky.

5. Change the contents to the `Example 1 (InkVariables.ink)` file.

6. Save the file and return to Unity.

> **Reminder**
>
> The automatic recompilation of ink source files can be changed by visiting the **Project Settings** window. You can do this by clicking on **Edit** and then **Project Settings**. Clicking on **Ink** and then changing the **Compile All Ink Automatically** setting allows you to update this value. If enabled, the plugin will automatically create a JSON file.

7. Create a new, empty game object and name it `InkStory`.

8. Create a new `Script` component in the `InkStory` game object and name the new C# file `InkStoryScript.cs`.

9. Open the `InkStoryScript.cs` file for editing in Visual Studio.

10. Update the `InkStoryScript.cs` file to `Example 1 (InkStoryScript.cs)`.

    The updated code uses the `GetVariableWithName()` method as part of the `VariablesState` object. The `variablesState` property is used with the name of the variable in ink, `number_example`, as part of the `GetVariableWithName()` method. Additionally, the `Debug.Log()` method is used to display the value of the variable in the **Console** window when run in Unity.

11. Associate the file with the code. You can do this using either the **Select TextAsset** window or by dragging and dropping the compiled JSON file into the new `Ink JSON File` property inside the `Script` component.

12. Run the project in Unity.

Once the project starts running, open the **Console** window. A new message will have been added:

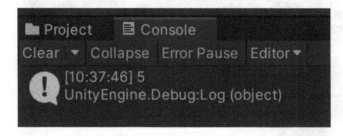

Figure 8.2 – The console window showing the value of the ink variable

13. Stop the running project in Unity.

If variables are defined before the first text content in ink, they are also loaded *before* the content. In *Example 1*, as is evident from *Step 8*, the initial values of the variables can be accessed immediately after loading an ink story. The functionality for accessing variables is separate from the functionality of loading and displaying text content.

Any ink variable that is able to be accessed can also be changed. In the next section, we will discover how this functionality is key to using the `variablesState` property, as part of the Ink API, and how it allows you to create more complex projects in Unity when using the ink-Unity Integration plugin.

Changing the value of the ink variables

The English word "variable" means *able to be changed*. All ink variables, once created, can be changed at any point. The `variablesState` property follows the same pattern. If a variable can be accessed, its value can be changed.

The `VariablesState` class contains multiple methods in which to access and change the values of the variables within an ink story. However, it also contains a shorthand access operator using square brackets and the name of the variable in quotation marks. Often, this shorthand is used rather than directly using method names to change the values of variables within the `variablesState` property.

Now, return to the project that we used as part of the *Accessing Ink variables* section. Perform the following steps:

1. Open the `InkStoryScript.cs` file for editing in Visual Studio.
2. Change the existing code to `Example 2` (`InkStoryScript.cs`).

3. Save the file and return to Unity.

4. Run the project.

The **Console** window will show an updated message. Instead of showing the initial value of the variable, it will show an updated value:

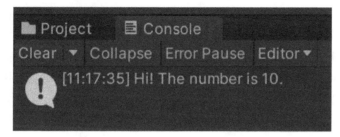

Figure 8.3 – The updated value of the ink variable in the Console window

Once a story has been loaded, the values of its variables exist within the variablesState property. Any changes to these values are reflected in the next use of the Continue() or ContinueMaximally() methods.

5. Stop the running project in Unity.

Variables are not the only values that can be accessed from outside an ink story. The ink-Unity Integration plugin also adds the ability to call functions in ink from Unity. While accessing and changing the values of variables can be helpful, directly calling functions in ink and passing them values from Unity is often the preferred way in which to approach the exchange of data between Unity and ink. In the next section, we will review why using functions is frequently the better option for complex data or for when you want to process multiple values as part of the same task in ink.

Calling ink functions externally

As with variables, functions are also global in ink. This means they can be accessed as part of any ink code that is part of the same story. As part of the Unity API provided by the Story class, the EvaluateFunction() method calls a function in the ink code based on the name passed to it. Because functions in ink are global, they can be called from outside the story itself. However, unlike working with the variablesState property and only accessing a single value, multiple values can be passed to an ink function at one time. Additionally, the EvaluateFunction() method can be configured to return the text output within the ink function or any returning data, too.

In this section, we will begin by testing whether an ink function exists using the `HasFunction()` method. Next, we will examine how the `EvaluateFunction()` method is the preferred option for complex data or multiple data values when communicating between Unity and ink. Finally, we will review examples of how to use the text result and return data from an ink function within Unity code.

Verifying and evaluating ink functions

When working with functions in ink, the `HasFunction()` method verifies whether an ink function exists. Note that it should always be used before working with an ink function to prevent any issues:

1. Create a new project in Unity based on the built-in 2D template.

2. Import the ink-Unity Integration plugin.

3. Create a new, empty game object named `InkStory`.

4. Add a `Script` component to the `InkStory` game object and name the ink file `InkStoryFunctions.cs`.

5. Add a new ink file and rename it `InkFunctions.ink`.

6. Open the `InkFunctions.ink` file in Inky and change its contents to `Example 4 (InkFunctions.ink)`.

7. Open `InkStoryFunctions.cs` for editing in Visual Studio.

8. Update the `InkStoryFunctions.cs` file to `Example 4 (InkStoryFunctions.cs)`.

9. Save the `InkStoryFunctions.cs` file.

10. In Unity, associate the compiled JSON file for the `InkFunctions.ink` file with the `Ink JSON File` property, as part of the `Script` component of the `InkStory` game object.

11. Run the project.

    In the **Console** window, a message will appear, showing how the `relationship` ink variable has been changed as a result of calling two methods, `HasFunction()` and `EvaluateFunction()`. The `HasFunction()` method of the `Story` class returns a Boolean value. It also guarantees that a function exists before it is used.

12. Stop the project.

After verifying that a function exists, it can be evaluated. The code in the `InkStoryFunctions.cs` file uses two methods: `HasFunction()` and `EvaluateFunction()`. Within the ink API, the term **evaluate** is important. Functions in ink are a special form of knots, which means they are sections of a story. This potentially means that any usage of ink functions can be incredibly disruptive to the existing values in the story. The term **evaluate** informs the developer how the result of the action of working with a function might change existing values. In ink, functions are *evaluated* using the `EvaluateFunction()` method.

When using the `EvaluateFunction()` method, the first parameter is the name of the function in ink. Any additional parameters are passed to the ink function directly. In the code that is used as part of the `InkStoryFunctions.cs` file, the use of the `EvaluateFunction()` method includes two parameters: the name of the `increase()` ink function and the amount of value to increase inside ink.

This use of an ink function that has been called from Unity to change values is a very common pattern when using the ink-Unity Integration plugin. In this case, the `increase()` function in ink updates the `relationship` value inside ink. This allows ink values to be adjusted by ink functions. When working in Unity, values can be passed to ink to perform multiple tasks, depending on the ink functions defined for those tasks, without extra code on the Unity side.

ink functions are special sections of a story. This means they can also produce text output along with other code-related actions. However, to gain access to the text output of an ink function using the `EvaluateFunction()` method, a special keyword is needed in C#: `out`. We will learn more about this keyword in the next section.

Retrieving the ink function text output

The C# programming language allows you to define a variable and then pass it to a method. Internal to the method, it is expected that the value of the variable will change. Note that this will not be a change to the value passed to the method, but to the value contained within the variable itself. More generally, in programming, this is known as passing by reference. Instead of passing some data to a method, a reference (that is, where to find the variable to store the value) is passed instead.

In C#, the `out` keyword can be used with a parameter to a method to specify that the variable, and not its value, should be passed by reference. This means that when the method is finished with its actions, the value within a variable that was passed to the method will change as a result. In C#, using the `out` keyword allows a developer to specify they want a value *out* of the method and into a specific variable.

When working with the `EvaluateFunction()` method provided by the ink-Unity Integration plugin, if the second parameter uses the `out` keyword, the method knows to take any text produced during the evaluation and pass it *out* of the method back to the variable. Perform the following steps:

1. Return to the code used in the *Verifying and evaluating ink functions* section.
2. Update the code in the `InkStoryFunctions.cs` file to Example 5 (`InkStoryFunctions.cs`).
3. Save the changed `InkStoryFunctions.cs` file.
4. Return to Unity.
5. Play the project.
6. Stop the project.

Using the `out` keyword with the `functionOut` variable as a parameter to the `EvaluateFunction()` method lets C# know to pass any text *out* of the method. Because the `relationship` value was updated internally in ink by calling the `increase()` function from Unity to ink, its value is shown as `51` in the **Console** window when the project is run. The `functionOut` variable in C# is given the text *out* of the use of the `EvaluateFunction()` method. This allows it to then pass its value to the `Debug.Log()` method and, ultimately, show the updated value in the **Console** window.

When the `out` keyword is used with the `EvaluateFunction()` method in this way, any text output from a function can be captured and passed back from ink to Unity. Combined with creating ink functions to update ink values, this additional change to the pattern shown in the *Verifying and evaluating ink functions* section allows you to call ink functions to perform ink-related tasks. This allows for the separation between ink concerns and those in Unity.

Within ink, a story can be controlled by different values. Using conditional options and a selective output, the text of a choice can be displayed or a diversion followed. Because the values of variables can be directly accessed using the `variablesState` property and functions that have been called using the `EvaluateFunction()` method, this means an ink story can be controlled from Unity. In the next section, we will learn how to connect user interface elements in Unity with ink variables and functions.

Controlling a story through variables and functions

The `variablesState` property and the `EvaluateFunction()` method give the developer two ways in which to access values within an ink story. By using these two approaches, a story can be *controlled* by more than just the options that are presented to a player. User interface elements within Unity can be attached to methods that can then change ink values.

In this section, we will connect ink to Unity. By using the `variablesState` property and the `EvaluateFunction()` method, we will review a code pattern where Unity provides the user interface and communicates with ink functions to adjust and react to values during runtime.

Across the three sections of this topic, first, we will prepare a Unity project by creating the necessary game objects. Next, we will add the code to control the user interface. Finally, we will adjust the presentation of the user interface and run the project.

Preparing a user interface

To begin work with Unity buttons, a new project is required. For simplicity, a 2D project is recommended. This will allow you to work easily with an interface without needing to worry about perspective. Perform the following steps:

1. Create a new project in Unity using the built-in 2D template and name this project `Shopping Trip`.

2. Import the ink-Unity Integration plugin.

3. Create a new, empty game object named `InkStory`.

4. Create a new `Script` component inside the `InkStory` game object. Name the created C# file `InkStoryShopping.cs`.

5. Create a new ink file named `InkShopping.ink`.

6. Open the `InkShopping.ink` file for editing in Inky and change its contents to `Example 6 (InkShopping.ink)`.

In Unity, create a new `Button` game object. Select the automatically created `Canvas` game object in Unity and create a second `Button` game object so that both buttons are the children of the `Canvas` game object:

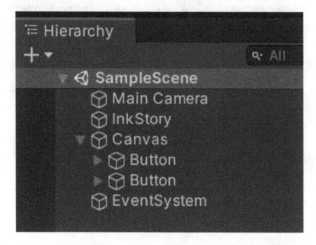

Figure 8.4 – The created buttons in Unity

7. Select the `Canvas` game object again and create a `Text` game object. Both buttons, along with the newly created `Text` game object, should all be children of the `Canvas` game object.

The ink file created as part of *Step 6* established the ink functions that will be called from future Unity code. The two buttons will serve as an interface for the buying and selling of an inventory that is also tracked by the ink code. In the next section, we will move from having set up everything to writing the Unity code to create a bridge between the interface and ink. This will track two values: `money` and `inventory`.

Scripting user interface objects

In the previous section, we worked through the steps that were needed to create a new Unity 2D project and to create the necessary game objects. In this section, we will learn how to connect user actions (that is, clicking) with the user interface by adding code on the Unity side. Then, we will use the `EvaluateFunction()` method in Unity to communicate with ink functions within a running story to control its progression:

1. Open the `InkStoryShopping.cs` file for editing in Visual Studio.

2. Change its content to `Example 6 (InkStoryShopping.cs)`.

In the new code, three new methods have been added to the Unity code. We have directly mapped the Unity methods to ink functions. For example, the name of the Sell() method in Unity almost matches the sell() name of the ink function. The differences in capitalization are only because of the recommended capitalization usage in each programming context.

3. Associate the compiled ink JSON file with the new public property. Associate the Text game object with the Text Status property:

Figure 8.5 – Associating the Text GameObject with the Text Status property

> **Recommendation**
>
> Because the two existing Button game objects have children Text game objects, it is recommended that you use the drag-and-drop approach to associate a game object with a property. This will prevent any issues with associating the wrong Text game object.

4. Select the Canvas game object in Unity in the **Hierarchy** view. In the **Inspector** view, click on **Add Component**, **Layout**, and then **Horizontal Layout Group**. This will add a Horizontal Layout Group component.

5. Change the **Child Alignment** property of the `Horizontal Layout Group` component from the default value of **Upper Left** to **Middle Center**:

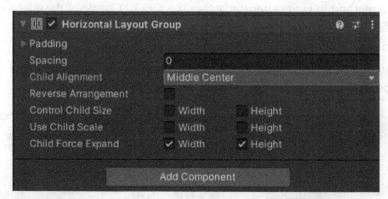

Figure 8.6 – The adjusted Child Alignment property for Horizontal Layout Group

The addition of the `Horizontal Layout Group` component adds a layout structure to the `Canvas` game object. The adjustment of the **Child Alignment** property changes the starting position of all its children to the absolute-center positions of the available screen space.

6. Select the first `Button` game object of the children game objects of the `Canvas` game object, in the **Hierarchy** view, in Unity. In the **Inspector** view, scroll down to the **On Click ()** component. At the bottom of this area, click on the small plus (+) symbol:

Figure 8.7 – Addition to the On Click () component

Each `Button` game object can have one or more listener functions associated with its `OnClick` user event. When a user clicks on the `Button` game object, these functions will be called in the order in which they appear in the list.

Because Button is a GameObject, it can only communicate with other game objects. This is an important aspect of how Unity understands the differences between game objects and their components. A GameObject is a *container* for other components, including any script components. This means that to connect the OnClick user event for a Button game object to some code found in a script component, the GameObject that the script component is associated with must be used. For us, this means the InkStory game object.

7. Associate the InkStory game object with the On Click () component of the first Button game object. This can be done by dragging and dropping the InkStory game object onto the property:

Figure 8.8 – Associating the InkStory GameObject with the On Click () component

Once a GameObject has been associated with an entry in the On Click () component listing, the **No Function** drop-down menu will be enabled. Upon this association, Unity will have processed the game object and looked for every possible method or function that might be used.

8. Using the **No Function** drop-down menu, select the **InkStoryShopping** object and then the **Buy ()** method entry.

Once the method has been associated as a listening function, the value of the **No Function** drop-down menu will update to InkStoryShopping.Buy.

9. Select the second Button game object of the children of the Canvas game object, in the **Hierarchy** view, in Unity. In the **Inspector** view, scroll down to the On Click () component.

10. Follow *Step 7* and *Step 8* to associate the `InkStory` game object with the `On Click ()` component. For *Step 8*, instead of using the `Buy ()` method, select the `Sell ()` method:

Figure 8.9 – Associating the InkStoryShopping.Sell() method

At the end of *Step 10*, the first `Button` game object is associated with the `Buy ()` method, and the second is associated with the `Sell ()` method. Internally, those methods are communicating with their corresponding ink functions. As you will discover shortly, clicking on the buttons will call Unity methods, which, in turn, will call ink functions.

Adjusting the presentation values

In this final section, we will change the default values of the user interface game objects created in the previous section. Adjusting these values will help us to better understand the relationship between game objects and improve the experience of interacting with the onscreen buttons:

1. Select the first `Button` game object in the **Hierarchy** view in Unity. Using the drop-down arrow next to its name, expand the listing of these children and click on the first `Text` game object.

2. Change the `Text` property value from its default setting of `Button` to `Buy`:

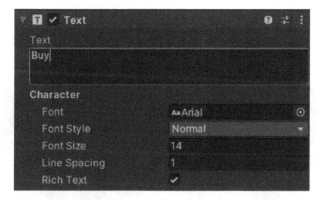

Figure 8.10 – Changing the Text property

3. Select the second Button game object in the **Hierarchy** view in Unity. Using the drop-down arrow next to its name, expand the listing of these children and click on the first Text game object presented.

4. Change the default text of the second Button game object from Button to Sell.

5. Select the third child game object of the Canvas game object, that is, the Text game object. Be sure not to select the previous two Text game objects that were updated in the previous steps.

6. Change the width and height of the Text game object to 400 and 250:

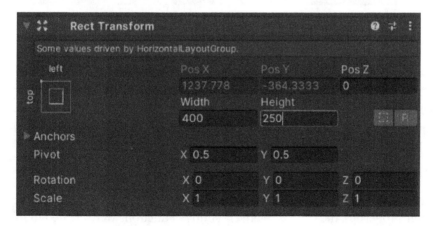

Figure 8.11 – Adjusting the width and height of the Text game object

7. Change the font size of the Text game object from its default value to 32.

8. Change the color of the Text game object from its default setting to a white or near-white color:

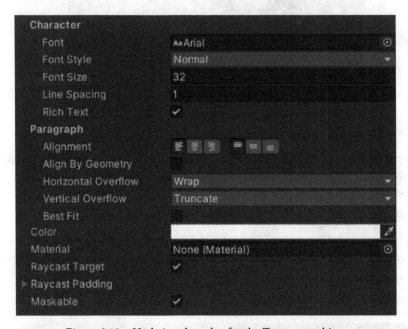

Figure 8.12 – Updating the color for the Text game object

9. Play the project.

    When played, the far-left side will show the updated status of the money and inventory variables in ink. Clicking on the buttons will call the Unity methods, which, in turn, will evaluate the ink functions and change the values inside the running ink story. This is a complete example of how to *control* an ink story through variables and functions.

10. Stop the project.

While multiple steps were involved to create the user interface elements and change the values of their properties, the code is relatively simple. Functions were created in ink to adjust the ink values. In Unity, methods were created matching the names of the ink functions.

This section demonstrated how a simple shopping scene could be created in ink and manipulated from Unity. By knowing the name of the ink functions, C# methods in Unity can evaluate them to either adjust values or, in the case of the `status()` ink function, retrieve the text output. This was also a demonstration of how to separate user interface programming from story-related code. They communicated with each other, but they were written in different contexts.

In the next chapter, we will examine a different approach to working with variables and functions in a story while continuing the trend of separating our narrative and game code. However, instead of clicking on buttons in Unity to trigger functions in ink, we will explore the reverse. Events will happen in ink and trigger changes in Unity. This chapter focused on how to control ink from Unity. The next chapter will demonstrate how to control parts of Unity from events happening within a running ink story.

Summary

In this chapter, we began by demonstrating how the `variablesState` property exposes all of the variables in ink. We started by using the `GetVariableWithName()` method to access variables by name and the provided shorthand syntax of using square brackets. For completeness, the `variablesState` property was explained. However, in most situations, ink functions should change ink values. This helps to keep any code working with those values existing within the ink story and is easier to maintain over time, and we closed the chapter on this same theme. Additionally, we explored how buttons in Unity can call their methods and then call ink functions. By using the `EvaluateFunction()` method, we can access the ink function in Unity to either pass data into the project or retrieve possible text output with the `out` keyword in C#.

In *Chapter 9, Story API – Observing and Reacting to Story Events*, we will emphasize the ink-Unity Integration plugin and its API by inspecting a different approach to the relationship between Unity and ink. Instead of using Unity methods to call ink functions, we will examine some patterns to control parts of Unity from ink. Instead of having to click on buttons in Unity to change values, ink will cause changes that will then register in Unity. For projects requiring more real-time feedback from ink, these patterns will be a preferred approach to those shown in this chapter using the `variablesState` property and the `EvaluateFunction()` method.

Questions

1. Are variables global in ink?

2. What effect does functions being global mean regarding how they are accessed in ink?

3. Do the `Continue()` and `ContinueMaximally()` methods affect the values of variables in ink?

4. What shorthand syntax does the `VariablesState` class provide to access variables based on their names?

5. Should the name of an ink function be used to test whether it exists before you attempt to access it?

6. How is the `out` C# keyword used with the `EvaluateFunction()` method as part of the Story API when working with the ink-Unity Integration plugin?

9

Story API – Observing and Reacting to Story Events

In this chapter, we will explore how changes in a running ink story can trigger events in Unity. We will learn how the `ObserveVariable()` and `ObserveVariables()` methods of the Story API, as provided by the ink-Unity Integration plugin, allow you to prepare functions to react to future events in Unity. We will begin by observing a single variable and then move on to learn how to watch multiple values.

In *Chapter 8, Story API – Accessing ink Variables and Functions*, the focus was on controlling an ink story by calling its functions and changing its values from Unity. This chapter reverses the emphasis between the two systems. In this chapter, we will explore how narrative events, such as variables changing because of a player's choices, can be used to control what information is presented in Unity.

In this chapter, we will cover the following topics:

- Listening for variable changes
- Dynamically responding to ink stories
- Observing multiple ink values

Technical requirements

The examples used in this chapter, in the `*.ink` files, can be found on GitHub at `https://github.com/PacktPublishing/Dynamic-Story-Scripting-with-the-ink-Scripting-Language/tree/main/Chapter9`.

Listening for variable changes

Variables in ink are global. Once they are created, they can be accessed at any point in the story. In *Chapter 8*, *Story API – Accessing ink Variables and Functions*, we learned how this functionality can be used with the `variablesState` property to access or change their values. However, instead of directly interfering in a running ink from Unity, we can also wait for something to happen in ink and then react in Unity. The verb used for this type of approach, as part of the Story API, is called *observing*.

When we observe an ink variable, we can write our own rules regarding what should happen when its value changes or meets a certain threshold. We are merely *observing* its value. What we do because of this observance is up to the developer.

In this topic, we will explore the `ObserveVariable()` method.

> **Recommendation**
>
> It is recommended that you create a new Unity 2D project for this topic. Instructions regarding how to create a new Unity project and import the ink-Unity Integration plugin can be found in *Chapter 6*, *Adding and Working with the ink Unity Plugin*.

We will perform the following steps:

1. In a new Unity project, using the 2D template with the ink-Unity Integration plugin imported, create a new, empty game object and name it `InkStory`. This game object will hold the `script` component and react to changes in the Ink code.

2. Create a new Ink file and name it `InkStoryStepCounter.ink`.

3. Open `InkStoryStepCounter.ink` for editing in Inky and update its contents to `Example 1 (InkStoryStepCounter.ink)`.

4. Create a new `script` component inside the `InkStory` game object. Name the created file `InkStoryScript.cs`.

5. Open `InkStoryScript.cs` for editing in Visual Studio.

   Update `InkStoryScript.cs` to `Example 1 (InkStoryScript.cs)`.

   The `ObserveVariable()` method is a new method introduced in this chapter and accepts two parameters. The first parameter is the name of a variable to observe and the second is a function or a method to call.

   The code used in this example also incorporates a C# concept known as a **lambda expression**. Any function without a name in C# is a lambda expression. This allows you to write a function with its parameters and body, but without a name.

   Putting the concepts together, the `ObserveVariable()` method watches a variable in ink. If its value changes at any point, the lambda expression will run. This operates outside the normal flow.

6. Associate the compiled Ink JSON file.

7. Run the project.

When the project is run, the **Console** window will show a series of messages. The first message will show the text of the story, the second will show the value produced by the `ObserveVariable()` method, and the third will be the text produced as the first option chosen:

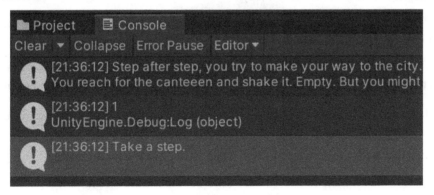

Figure 9.1 – The Text output is shown in order of execution in Unity

The reason why the second message shows the value before the third text of the option is because of the execution order. Within the running ink story, the ObserveVariable() method occurs *before* the text output is produced for the option and returned to Unity. The use of the delegated lambda expression occurs outside the normal flow of execution in this way. Whenever the value of the observed variable changes, the function is immediately called, regardless of any other code happening around it at the same time.

In the next section, we will build on this pattern. Often, there are contexts in which Unity should only be told a variable has been changed when it happens. This frees up the execution time for other tasks in Unity and allows a developer to write more reactive code that only runs when needed.

Dynamically responding to ink stories

In Unity, multiple methods are called as part of the normal execution cycle when a project runs. Often, methods such as Update(), a common part of behavior scripts in Unity, include many lines of code. Even a method such as FixedUpdate(), called at the end of the physics calculations for each cycle in a running project, might include multiple parts. Any code that depends on other systems, such as those communicating with ink, can also add extra time per cycle.

The use of the ObserveVariable() method allows data from ink to only update Unity when needed. Because the Story API will only call the delegated function when necessary, Unity will also only get the data when there is a change it needs to know about when it needs to know about it. This will also happen outside the use of an Update() method or even a FixedUpdate() method in Unity.

In this section, we will examine how the ObserveVariable() method operates outside of other methods as part of Unity. It will only call the delegated function when a value changes allowing a dynamic response in Unity.

Return to the project created in the previous section, and perform the following steps:

1. Update the InkStoryScript.cs file to Example 2 (InkStoryScript. cs).

2. Within the Update() method, four different actions are taking place.

    The *first* is the increase in the variable time with the most recent Time. deltaTime, which is the number of milliseconds between cycles as measured in a decimal (float) number. The *second* is a conversion between its float value into an integer. This operation removes the decimal part of the number. The *third* action is a mathematical operation called **modulo**.

In many programming languages, C# among them, the percentage symbol, %, can be used to find the remainder from division. This operation is called *modulo*. However, many programming languages also use the term *remainder operator*. When this operation is performed, it will determine how many times one number can be divided into another. In this case, using the remainder of 60, the seconds variable will always be equal to the number of seconds that have passed since the project began, as divided by the time variable.

The *fourth* action within the Update() method is the assignment of the seconds variable to the number of seconds, as defined by the previously explained actions. In every cycle in Unity, this number will be updated, and the seconds variable will always be up to date.

One final action takes place in the delegated function, that is, the use of the Destroy() method. Within the code, once the value of the steps ink variable is equal to 3, as determined by Unity, it will remove a button from the scene. This helps to keep the control of the button connected to a value changed outside of Unity. Once the ink variable changes and is reported to Unity, the button is removed.

On the last line of the Start() method, a button is given a listener function for its onClick event. When the button is clicked on, any functions associated with the listeners will be called. In this example, clicking on the button will call the new TakeStep() method. This will load the next text content up to the next weave encountered in the ink code and then choose the first (0) option within the weave. This will cause the ink code to loop internally.

With the code created, two more steps are required before the project can be played. First, a new Button game object needs to be added to the project. Then, once the Button game object exists, it must be associated with the InkStory property as part of the new code.

3. Create a new Button game object in Unity.

4. Associate the Button game object with the Button Step property.

5. Play the project.

6. The created Button game object appears at the bottom of the scene. Clicking on the Button game object four times will cause it to disappear, and a message will appear in the **Console** window:

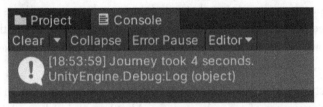

Figure 9.2 – A message in the Console window generated by a delegated function

7. Stop the project.

When the project first started, the Update() method of the code was called during each cycle. Internally, it updated the time and seconds variables in the Unity code. Whenever the Button game object was clicked on, it progressed the ink code, which looped itself internally. Because of the use of the ObserveVariable() method, any time the ink variable steps were updated, it called the delegated function and tested the new value passed to it. Once it reached 3 (based on a total of four clicks to move it from 0 to 3), the delegated function created a message in the **Console** window and destroyed the Button game object.

The example used in this section follows a common pattern where Unity performs its own calculations as part of a method, such as Update(), and dynamically responds to changes in an ink story as they happen. Instead of potentially checking the steps ink variable as part of the variablesState property every cycle, and wasting time if the value has not changed, the delegated function allows Unity to only act when needed. For more complicated projects, this is the preferred approach, and generally, it produces faster projects.

More than a single variable can be observed in ink. Depending on the complexity of design, a Unity project might be interested in observing multiple ink values and updating onscreen areas with information on story progression or the current statistics of the player. For these contexts, a different method is needed: ObserveVariables(). In the next section, we will demonstrate how to work with this method.

Observing multiple ink values

Along with the ObserveVariable() method is a sister method named
ObserveVariables(). However, while the ObserveVariable() method accepts
the name of a variable and a delegate function, the ObserveVariables() method
accepts an IList<string> of variable names and a delegate function. Instead of
responding when a single variable is changed, its delegate function is called when any of
the variables passed as a list to the method are changed. While slightly more complicated
to set up, the ObserveVariables() method provides the functionality to observe
multiple ink variables.

Recommendation

It is recommended that you create a new Unity 2D project for this section.
Instructions regarding how to create a new Unity project and import the
ink-Unity Integration plugin can be found in *Chapter 6, Adding and Working
with the ink-Unity Integration Plugin.*

Perform the following steps:

1. In a new Unity 2D project with the ink-Unity Integration plugin imported, create
    a new, empty game object and name it InkStory. This game object will hold the
    Script component and react to any changes in the ink code.

2. Create a new ink file and name it InkStoryPlayerStatistics.ink.

3. Open the InkStoryPlayerStatistics.ink file for editing in Inky and
    update its content to Example 3 (InkStoryPlayerStatistics.ink).

4. Create a new script component inside the InkStory game object. Name the
    created file InkStoryPlayerStatisticsScript.cs.

5. Open the created InkStoryPlayerStatisticsScript.cs file in Visual
    Studio. Update it to Example 3 (InkStoryPlayerStatisticsScript.cs).

    The updated code begins by setting up the Story API. It does this by creating a new
    object based on the Story class. Next, a List<string> is created. This is used
    as a *list* of the variable names based on their string values. After creating the list,
    two values are added to it in an order, based on the names of the mental_health
    and physcial_health ink variables. This created list is then passed to the
    ObserveVariables() method, and a second parameter, that is, a delegated
    function in the form of a lambda expression, is used.

The `Start()` method ends with a call to the created `ProgressStory()` method. Inside this created method, the story is progressed programmatically by using the `ContinueMaximally()` and `ChooseChoiceIndex()` methods. The first method loads all of the text content up to the first weave, while the second method selects the first (0) option in the weave. The final, second use of the `ContinueMaximally()` method loads the resulting text within the Ink code and is needed to cause the variable to change.

6. Associate the compiled Ink JSON file with the `InkStory` game object.

7. Run the project.

When the project starts, it will programmatically progress the ink story used within this section. As a result, it will produce a message in the **Console** window:

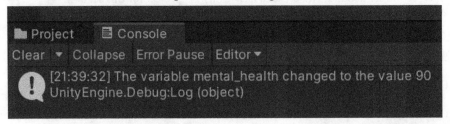

Figure 9.3 – The Console window showing changes to the mental_health ink variable

Two different ink variables were added to the `List<string>` that was passed to the `ObserveVariables()` method. However, only one of them was changed because of the ink story progression. As a result, the variable changed, and its new value was passed back to Unity. When the change happened, the delegated function was called with the second parameter, the name of the variable (`variableName`), and its new value (`newValue`).

The `ObserveVariables()` method works similarly to its sister `ObserveVariable()` method. Both respond with the name of the variable and the changed value as soon as they happen in ink. The major difference between them is in their first parameter. The `ObserveVariables()` method accepts the name of a single variable name in ink, and the `ObserveVariables()` method is a list of which variables to observe and then respond to using the delegated function.

8. Stop the project.

This section focused on the use of the ObserveVariables() method, echoing the pattern in the previous section where we used the ObserveVariable() sister method. In general, either approach offers a way to control how Unity reacts to ink, shifting the control of information between the two systems. Along with the variablesState property, the different approaches in this chapter, as covered in *Chapter 8, Story API – Accessing ink Variables and Functions*, provide access to the variables in ink. They can be used in a project, depending on the needs of the developer, to either drive a Unity project more from the ink side or directly change values on the ink side from the Unity code as needed.

Summary

In this chapter, we explored multiple examples. First, we started with the ObserveVariable() method and watched only one variable. In the second section, we dynamically responded to ink stories in Unity. Using delegated functions, we learned how parts of a piece of code will only be called when an ink variable changes. In the third section, we looked at the use of the ObserveVariables() method to watch multiple variables specified by name.

In *Chapter 10, Dialogue Systems with ink*, we will move away from the individual properties and methods of the Story API and start to combine functionality into more complex use cases. Combining parts of the Unity API introduced in *Chapter 7, Unity API – Making Choices and Story Progression*, along with the ObserveVariable() method covered in this chapter, we will examine how to create different dialogue systems.

Questions

1. What is the action of *observing*, and how does it apply to the methods provided by the Story class?

2. What roles do delegated functions serve when working with the ObserveVariable() and ObserveVariables() methods?

3. What is the difference between the ObserveVariable() method and the ObserveVariables() method?

4. What is the difference between accessing ink variables using the variablesState property and using the ObserveVariable() method or the ObserveVariables() method?

Section 3: Narrative Scripting with ink

By the time you've completed this chapter, you will have code examples of dialogue, quest, and simple procedural storytelling systems using ink and its Story API in Unity. This section contains the following chapters:

- *Chapter 10, Dialogue Systems with ink*
- *Chapter 11, Quest Tracking and Branching Narratives*
- *Chapter 12, Procedural Storytelling with ink*

10
Dialogue Systems with ink

In this chapter, we will explore three different approaches to create a **dialogue system** using ink, Unity, and the ink-Unity Integration plugin. In the first topic, we will begin by examining how **hashtags**, that is, text content starting with a hash (#), can be used to mark different lines in ink as being associated with certain characters in a story. Then, we will discuss an alternative to tags, where the name of the speaker precedes their dialogue. Finally, we will conclude the first part by reviewing how tags can be used and how both approaches can be combined.

In the second topic, we will look at how to recreate the **click-to-continue** dialogue pattern that is found in many video games using ink. We will explore various ways of saving time and effort by using tunnels to move to different knots and back again in an ink project for use when needed. Following this, we will examine several different ways in which to generate dialogue trees in ink where players can explore different paths through extended branches of conversation.

In the third and final topic, we will look at two common visual patterns in which to present dialogue options to players, that is, lists and radial menus, and how they affect both writing ink code and how information is displayed to a player in Unity. We will begin with the visual pattern of a list, where all options are shown to the player in a vertical pattern. Then, we will examine the **radial menu pattern**, where options are limited to a smaller number of options arranged in a specific, visual way.

In this chapter, we will cover the following topics:

- Writing dialogue in ink using tags
- Dialogue loops and story knots
- User interface models for conversations

> **Note**
>
> Unlike previous chapters, where sections built toward a completed project, this chapter will examine different approaches toward more visually complex systems. Each approach covered by a section can be found online on GitHub as a completed project. Only selected files and code, as they relate to the approach of each section, will be shown in this chapter. The specific files of each example are also noted within each section.

Technical requirements

The completed code for the different sections of this chapter can be found on GitHub at `https://github.com/PacktPublishing/Dynamic-Story-Scripting-with-the-ink-Scripting-Language/tree/main/Chapter10`.

Writing dialogue in Ink using tags

When ink was first introduced in *Chapter 1*, *Text, Flow, Choices, and Weaves*, the importance of a single line was also discussed. Each line in ink can consist of code, text, or a combination of the two. Depending on the use of other concepts, such as glue or comments, what counts as a single line can often be composed of multiple blocks of text or include notes for the authors as part of a single line. However, in addition to these previously reviewed concepts is another concept that has not previously been discussed: **hashtags**.

In ink, a new, single *hashtag* is created when a hash (#) is used before any text. Starting from the hash (#) and until the end of that line, any text that appears between the two is considered part of the single *tag*:

```
This is text. #This is a tag.
```

Hashtags in ink are specifically designed to work with other systems. They have no meaning within Inky itself and are shown in the middle of the output:

This is text.

```
# This is a tag.
```

End of story

Figure 10.1 – A hashtag used within Inky

When working with another system such as Unity, hashtags can be used to add extra data to a single line in ink. The current tags for the loaded chunk of the ink story exist within a property provided by the Story API, called `currentTags`, which contains a `List<string>` of all tags detected within the last load of story content. As with other text-related content, the `currentTags` property is also affected by any usages of the `Continue()` or `ContinueMaximally()` methods.

We will begin by learning how to use hashtags in ink. We will retrieve their values using the `currentTags` property in Unity to build a simple dialogue system where each spoken line has a name associated with who is communicating it. Next, we will examine a different approach to the same dialogue system using speech tags in front of the text of each ink line. The last section of this topic will compare the two approaches and review when one might be better than the other or whether a combination of the two might be needed.

Tagging ink text

In ink, hashtags are used on a per-line basis. They exist for that line but remain part of the current hashtags until the next part of the story is loaded using the `Continue()` or `ContinueMaximally()` methods. In this section, we will review an example that uses hashtags with dialogue and the name of the speaker as part of a single line in ink. We will learn how the `currentTags` property is affected using the `Continue()` and `ContinueMaximally()` methods.

> **Reminder**
> The completed project for this section can be found in the *Chapter 10* examples on GitHub; these are under the name of *Chapter10-TaggingInkText*. Only selected parts of the code will be shown as they relate to the concepts examined in this section.

Dialogue lines are meaningless unless attributed to a character within a piece of work. This helps establish who is communicating and enables you to build continuity within the story. In the `Chapter10-TaggingInkText` example, each line of dialogue ends with the name of its speaker as a hashtag in ink. This helps attribute who is communicating each line:

Example 1 (InkDialogueTags.ink):

```
Hi, there! Welcome to an Ink example! #???
* [\[Continue\]]
-
My name is Narrator! I will be guiding you through this
example.
.. #Narrator
* [\[Continue\]]
-
My name is Dan. #Dan
* [\[Continue\]]
-
I'm another character in this example! #Dan
```

The ink code of *Example 1* contains the lines of dialogue and the name of the speaker for each line. Moving over to Unity, this translates into using the `currentTags` property to access the tags after at least one use of the `Continue()` or `ContinueMaximally()` methods:

Example 2 (InkStoryScript.cs):

```
void UpdatePanel()
{
DestroyChildren(OptionsPanel.transform);
InkOutputText.text = InkStory.ContinueMaximally();
SpeakerNameText.text = InkStory.currentTags[0];
}
```

In *Example 2*, because the `currentTags` property is a `List<string>`, the first (0) position can be retrieved using the number of its index. The result is the separation of the tagged speaker and their lines in Unity despite them being written as one line in ink.

Hashtags are a powerful tool in which to add extra data to a single line in ink. As demonstrated in this section, they can be used to add the name of the character communicating the line at the end each time. However, there is another way to achieve the same outcome. In the next section, we will repeat the same general code but use *speech tags* in front of each line instead.

Using speech tags

In creative writing, a **speech tag** appears before or after some dialogue and signals who is doing the communicating. For example, a common example found in many novels might use the word *said* in the following way:

```
"Hello," Dan said.
```

The use of *Dan said* acts as a *tag* to the speech captured in the quotation marks. It signals who is doing the talking (*Dan*) and what is being said (*Hello*).

Often, many people who write for games or other interactive projects follow a slightly different format where the name of the speaker appears before the speech. This style borrows from conventions found in screenwriting. The same words used in the previous example might appear as follows:

```
Dan: Hello
```

In the updated form, the use of quotation marks is dropped, and the name of the speaker precedes their words. There is also an introduction of a colon (:). This marks the end of the speaker and the beginning of their words. In screenwriting, both the name of the speaker and their dialogue will be centered. However, in an updated form that is more commonly used as part of game writing, this formatting is dropped, and the text appears as part of one line.

> **Reminder**
>
> The completed project for this section can be found inside the *Chapter 10* examples on GitHub under the name of `Chapter10-UsingSpeechTags`. Only selected parts of the code will be shown as they relate to the concepts examined in this section.

The ink code in `Chapter10-UsingSpeechTags` follows a different pattern from the one found in the previous section. Instead of the name of the speaker included as a hashtag after the dialogue lines, it now precedes it. Often, this format is used for dialogue by writers working on video games and other interactive projects:

Example 3 (InkSpeechTags.ink):

```
???: Hi, there! Welcome to an Ink example!
* [\[Continue\]]

-
Narrator: My name is Narrator! I will be guiding you through
this example.
* [\[Continue\]]

-
Dan: My name is Dan.
* [\[Continue\]]

-
Dan: I'm another character in this example!
```

When the *Example 3* code is run in Inky, because the code is no longer using hashtags, the first output and weave will be updated:

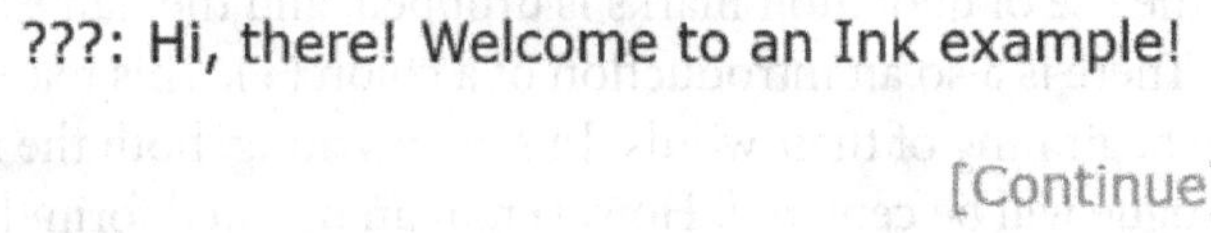

???: Hi, there! Welcome to an Ink example!

[Continue]

Figure 10.2 – Speech tag usage in Inky

Immediately, there is a visual difference between using ink hashtags and formatting the dialogue using speech tags. When testing the code in Inky, it is obvious who is communicating because their name will precede the text. However, while testing in Inky is easier, the removal of the hashtags within the ink code means the `currentTags` property cannot be used. Instead, more C# code must be added to parse the name from each line of text.

To detect, parse, and remove the use of the colon (:) within the ink output, multiple lines of C# code are needed:

Example 4 (InkStoryScript.cs):

```csharp
void UpdatePanel()
{
DestroyChildren(OptionsPanel.transform);

string inkOutput = InkStory.ContinueMaximally();
if(inkOutput.Contains(":"))
{
string[] splitInkOutput = inkOutput.Split(':');
splitInkOutput[0] = splitInkOutput[0].TrimEnd(':');
SpeakerNameText.text = splitInkOutput[0];
InkOutputText.text = splitInkOutput[1];
}
else
{
SpeakerNameText.text = "";
InkOutputText.text = inkOutput;
}
}
```

Example 4 now detects whether a colon (:) exists in the output using the Contains() method. If it does, the string is split into two parts using the Split() method. The colon (:) is then trimmed from the first (0) string using the Trim() method and its value is then used for the speaker's name. The second (1) string is used for the output of Ink.

The result of this new code appears to be the same as the previous section. However, it uses speech tags to mark who is speaking and when. This makes it easier to test the ink code outside of Unity, as hashtags in ink have no meaning in Inky. However, this approach also comes with the issue that a colon (:) can *only* appear as part of the speech tag. If the text contains a colon, the C# code might become confused and attempt to split the text as though it contained a speech tag instead.

In the next section, we will compare each of the approaches outlined earlier:

- The *first* approach, using hashtags in ink, allows us to add extra data to a single line and then use the `currentTags` property to retrieve this in the C# code.

- The *second* approach, using speech tags directly in the text, makes the ink code easier to test but creates a need for more C# code to parse the resulting ink.

As we will mention in the next section, there might be contexts in which both approaches can be combined.

Reviewing approaches to tagging dialogue

In ink, hashtags add extra data per line. They can be used, as we learned in the *Tagging ink text* section, to add hashtags to each line of dialogue and then retrieve this data using the `currentTags` property in C# code as part of a Unity project. However, hashtags in ink come with two issues. The first is that they can only be used *per line*. The second is that only *one tag per line* can be used at a time. This makes hashtags very useful, for example, in the task of adding who is communicating to the line, but it also means they can only be used once per line.

Dialogue can be directly marked using speech tags in the text. As we learned in the *Using speech tags* section, a colon can be used to mark who the speaker is and what they are communicating. This can be very useful for testing in Inky, as the speaker and their lines are closely connected and appear together. However, using speech tags in ink requires additional C# code to understand the output. Additionally, it means the colon can only be used as part of speech tags, as any other user might create confusion.

Both approaches have benefits and potential obstacles when used separately. However, there are also contexts in which both approaches might be combined to present the name of the speaker using speech tags and to convey extra data using a tag in ink at the same time. For example, many games not only present text to a player but also use audio, video, or some type of animation closely linked to the text itself. In these cases, the text could contain a speech tag and the ink code could also use tags to signal that additional media should be played as part of the combined delivery of the dialogue to a player.

For games with spoken dialogue lines, it is very common to use a database or a spreadsheet of the text line and its corresponding audio based on a naming convention as part of the same row. Depending on the team, company, and other factors, the naming convention might use specific formatting or numbers, but a general example might include the type of audio, the character's name, their state of mind or emotion, and any additional information for the context, level, or area of the game:

```
dialogue_diana_happy_desert.mp3
```

Because ink hashtags can add extra data, a single line within the ink code can use speech tags to mark who was communicating and then use the hashtag after the line with the media file to play. Such code will combine both approaches.

> **Reminder**
>
> The completed project for this section can be found inside the *Chapter 10* examples on GitHub under the name of `Chapter10-CombiningTags`. Only selected parts of the code will be shown as they relate to the concepts examined in this section.

The ink code in the `Chapter10-CombiningTags` example uses the combined approach. It includes both the name of the speaker preceding the dialogue lines and the use of a hashtag with the corresponding media file or reference to be used when the line is shown:

Example 5 (InkCombiningTags.ink):

```
Diana: I love the desert! #dialogue_diana_happy_desert
* [\[Continue\]]

-

Diana: But I hate how hot it gets! #dialogue_diana_sad_desert
* [\[Continue\]]

-

Diana: Perhaps I'm just fickle. #dialogue_diana_shrug_desert
* [\[Continue\]]

-
```

For simplicity, the project for this section only displays the text of the hashtag. By adding an extra `Text` game object and associating it with an existing property, the adjusted C# code will incorporate the changes to parsing speech tags along with the usage of the `currentTags` property:

Example 6 (InkStoryScript.cs):

```
if(InkStory.currentTags.Count > 0)
{
MediaText.text = InkStory.currentTags[0];
}
```

```
else
{
MediaText.text = "";
}
```

In *Example 6*, the new code tests for the number of entries in the `currentTags` property. If it contains at least one hashtag, the first (0) entry is used as text for a `Text` game object. When run, the project shows the speaker, their communication, and the name of the media file that will be played or used as part of the dialogue in a smaller font.

In the next topic, we will recreate some common patterns found in video game dialogue. We will learn how to create a click-to-continue pattern as well as more complex dialogue trees for players to explore. There will also be advice for those starting new projects on how to plan and then allow the code in ink to guide you to create an interface in Unity.

Dialogue loops and story knots

Writing dialogue in ink often means being aware of how it will be used with other systems. In the previous section, we investigated two approaches to using tags when writing single lines of dialogue. In this topic, we will move away from a focus on individual lines and work with the larger structures within an ink project. By inspecting two common patterns in which to present choices to a player, we will learn how knots in ink can be reused within projects to save future time and effort. The last section in this topic also includes advice for starting a new project or converting it using ink.

Because it appears most often, we will begin with a pattern that appears in the *Writing dialogue in ink using tags* section as part of the ink code examples using tags: click to continue.

Click to continue

> **Reminder**
> The completed project for this section can be found inside the
> *Chapter 10* examples on GitHub under the name of `Chapter10-ClickToContinue`. Only selected parts of the code will be shown as they relate to the concepts examined in this section.

There are many repeating patterns found in video game writing. One of the most common is the **click-to-continue** pattern. This is the presentation of information across a series of messages to a player, where they must press a button or click on the screen to progress through them.

In ink, one way to create the click-to-continue pattern is with a single choice and then, usually, a gathering point to collapse the weave right after it. In its most simplistic form, it only contains these concepts and a single word to indicate an action, such as *Continue*:

```
*   [\[Continue\]]
-
```

Breaking out the click-to-continue code into a knot allows a writer to reuse the same section multiple times by writing it once and then tunneling to it and back again when needed. In an extended example, the use of a specific knot for this purpose saves more lines of code the more times it appears:

Example 7 (InkClickToContinue.ink):

```
Guard: Sir! A dragon! There's a dragon!
-> continue ->
King: What? Are you sure?
-> continue ->
Guard: Let me check!
-> continue ->
Guard: Just a large bird, turns out.
-> continue ->
Guard: Sorry, sir.
-> continue ->
== continue ==
+  [\[Continue\]]
-
->->
```

In the code for *Example 7*, the continue ink knot is reused multiple times. Each usage tunnels to the knot and returns. This allows the code to decrease the number of overall lines.

Based on the structure in ink, the amount of C# code can also be reduced. The pattern in the ink code can be reflected in a simplified technique in the C# code by providing a method and attaching to the overall panel holding two `Text` game objects:

Example 8 (InkStoryScript.cs):

```csharp
void UpdatePanel()
{
SpeakerNameText.text = "";
InkOutputText.text = "";


string inkOutput = "";

if (InkStory.canContinue)
{
inkOutput = InkStory.ContinueMaximally();
}

if (inkOutput.Contains(":"))
{
string[] splitInkOutput = inkOutput.Split(':');
splitInkOutput[0] = splitInkOutput[0].TrimEnd(':');
SpeakerNameText.text = splitInkOutput[0];
InkOutputText.text = splitInkOutput[1];
}
else
{
SpeakerNameText.text = "";
InkOutputText.text = inkOutput;
}
}
public void ProgressDialogue()
{
if(InkStory.currentChoices.Count > 0)
{
InkStory.ChooseChoiceIndex(0);
```

```
    }
UpdatePanel();
    }
```

In the new *Example 8* code, the `ProgressDialogue()` method is used by a `Panel` game object as part of an **EventTrigger** component:

Figure 10.3 – Event Trigger on the Panel game object

By associating the `ProgressDialogue()` method with the `Panel` game object, you can click on a visual representation of a dialogue. This then loads the next part of the click-to-continue pattern based on the ink code.

While the click-to-continue pattern is the most common, there is another, more advanced pattern found in many role-playing games and narrative-heavy interactive projects: dialogue trees. In this pattern, multiple options are presented with each expanding out to separate branches of dialogue for players to explore. In the next section, we will learn how to create this pattern in ink and how new options can be easily added to branches.

Counting choices for trees

In ink, a weave is composed of one or more choices. Depending on the code following each choice, multiple levels can be created, and the flow of an ink story can branch off into different paths. When it comes to presenting options, there are often contexts where a user will progress through what is known as a **dialogue tree**. The use of the word *tree* is named after the shape created by the different parts, or branches, with all of them together as a single trunk.

Often, in role-playing and narrative-heavy games, this pattern appears as part of a scene with information about an event or as part of a character explaining something to a player. In these scenarios, the normal use of weaves does not quite work as intended. Instead of needing to pick a single choice among a set, we need to progress *across* the collection instead. For this, a special built-in ink function is required: `CHOICE_COUNT()`.

The ink runtime keeps track of the current number of options within the loaded chunk. This number can be accessed as part of the CHOICE_COUNT() ink function. When used as part of a conditional option in ink, this allows an author to limit the number of options presented to a reader by comparing the current count with the value returned by the CHOICE_COUNT() function. However, to keep track of values across loops, a variable is required:

Example 9 (oneBranch.ink):

```
VAR count = 0
-> loop
== loop
~ count = CHOICE_COUNT()
* {limitChoice(count)} This is the first
* {limitChoice(count)} This is the second
* {limitChoice(count)} This is the third
+ Return
- -> loop
== function limitChoice(localCount) ==
~ return localCount == CHOICE_COUNT()
```

The use of the count variable in *Example 9* records the current choice count at the start of the loop. Then, for each choice in turn, the value is compared with the increased number of uses of the choice before the comparison. The effect is the loading of each choice, in turn, from the set. At the beginning of the loop, the This is the first option will be provided. The use of a gathering point will automatically loop the code. This will continue until there are no choices left except the sticky choice of Return. This last choice will always remain and allow the player to either close the dialogue or *return* to a previous point.

This model can be extended into multiple branches as well. For each tree, there needs to be a separate knot or stitch with tunnels used to move between to maintain the flow of the ink story. The use of multiple sections with their choice counts also means using another ink concept: temporary variables. The temp keyword can be used inside any knot or stitch to create a variable that does not exist outside of it:

Example 10 (multipleBranches.ink):

```
-> loop
== loop
```

```
<- tree1.branch1
<- tree1.branch2
+ \[Close\]
    -> DONE
- -> loop
== tree1
= branch1
~ temp count = CHOICE_COUNT()
* {limitChoice(count)} Branch 1, first
* {limitChoice(count)} Branch 1, second
* {limitChoice(count)} Branch 1, third
- -> loop
= branch2
~ temp count = CHOICE_COUNT()
* {limitChoice(count)} Branch 2, first
* {limitChoice(count)} Branch 2, second
* {limitChoice(count)} Branch 2, third
- -> loop
== function limitChoice(localCount) ==
~ return localCount == CHOICE_COUNT()
```

In the preceding code for *Example 10*, each branch is broken out into its own stitches within a larger collected knot. Starting with the `loop` knot, threads are used to pull in the two stitches and create a unified appearance of options from two different parts of the code.

Depending on the structure of the project, the CHOICE_COUNT() ink function can be used to limit one choice per set, in order, or a more traditional collection can be created. Each of these approaches provides different ways in which to create a dialogue tree for a player to explore. They can either exhaust each option one after another or use tunnels to pass the flow to the knot containing the tree structure and then back again.

In this section, we examined two different structures for dialogue systems: click-to-continue and dialogue trees. In the last topic in this chapter, we will finally transition from ink structures into their visual representations in Unity. We will examine two models for presenting options to users: lists and radial menus. We will determine when each is best used and how the models affect both the structures in ink and the designs in Unity.

User interface models for conversations

There is a long history of presenting dialogue options to players in video games and other interactive projects. From the earliest text prompts to complicated layers of menus in more modern video games, each generation of video game systems has introduced different methods of presenting information. However, two general models appear in many games: lists and radial menus. They can be explained as follows:

- Based on the original presentation of one choice after another in a vertical arrangement, the **list pattern** first appeared in early computer games and continues in visual designs where there is more space to show a variety of longer-text options to a player.

- The second model, the **radial menu pattern**, generally appears as part of role-playing games on video game consoles or mobile game spaces where there is limited visual space and, thus, options are arranged in a circle for easy access when using a controller.

In the first section, we will start with lists. As we have already mentioned in multiple Unity examples across this book, and in earlier topics in this chapter, the vertical arrangement of options is a very common approach. However, we will discuss some common pitfalls when using this model and review several examples where they are best used and others where you might want to avoid them before we move on to cover the radial menu model next.

Listing dialogue options

There is one question we should ask when considering the user interface model of a list: how much visual spacing is allowed for each option? In computer games focused on text or with narrative-heavy designs, the list model is often the best to use. However, the reason for this is based not on computer games themselves, but on the assumed input peripherals used with the system. Often, computer games use the mouse as a primary input. This means a user can click on various things and scroll through a long *list* of options. Because the user is accustomed to this form of input and is willing to move through a longer presentation of text, the list is often a great model to follow.

> **Reminder**
>
> The completed project for this section can be found in the *Chapter 10* examples on GitHub under the name of `Chapter10-ListingOptions`. Only selected parts of the code will be shown as they relate to the concepts examined in this section.

In some role-playing or visual novel-based video games, the player might be presented with many options based on their past associations with other characters, political parties, or organizations. The number of options might also be influenced by certain skills, traits, or other in-game perks that grant the player additional benefits within dialogue selection. The Chapter10-ListingOptions project is based on such a premise.

In the dialogue presented in the ink code, the player is aboard a passenger ship and on their way to another city where they encounter another character in a crew-only area. There are multiple programmed options for the player to consider, as follows:

Example 11 (InkListingOptions.ink):

```
You sneak into the crew-only area. After you close the door,
a man quickly stands up from what he was doing on the floor.
Behind him seems to be a corpse on the floor.
* "Just give me any money you have, and I won't tell the
captain you have been murdering on his ship."
* "Is that dark magic!? I'll go to report you to the captain
right now!"
* "I don't care what you are doing in here. Leave. Now."
* \[Necromancer\] "Praise the Bone Mother! What foul sorcery
have you been up to? And can I help?"
* "Oh, gosh. I totally forgot to clean up that body earlier. I
guess I must kill you now too."
* \[Ignore them.\]
```

Because of the amount of visual space taken up by the dialogue selection in the code for *Example 11*, the multiple options extend off the screen. The player must scroll down and carefully read over the list in order to consider their choice. Such an interface works well in visual designs with a heavy narrative focus or on platforms such as desktop computers where the user might feel comfortable reviewing everything before making a final decision when progressing through a dialogue tree. However, this is not the only model a developer might want to use.

In the next section, we will examine the radial menu pattern. Popularized by role-playing games on video game consoles where the number of inputs is limited, the radial menu pattern presents not only a design challenge but a writing one as well. As we will explore in more detail, the radial menu pattern limits the amount of text that appears on the screen and forces a developer to make sure the intent of a single word or phrase conveys the outcome the player will experience when choosing an option.

Presenting a radial menu for dialogue

Many video game controllers have at least one joystick and a limited number of buttons. Because of this reduced set of inputs, designing a user interface for a player to decide between multiple options often means presenting options arranged in a clockwise pattern on the screen. More commonly, this visual design pattern is called a **radial menu**. This term takes its name from the mathematical concept *radius*, which is the distance from the center of a circle to its perimeter. A *radial* menu shows options based on a circular pattern.

> **Reminder**
>
> The completed project for this section can be found in the *Chapter 10* examples on GitHub under the name of `Chapter10-OptionWheel`. Only selected parts of the code will be shown as they relate to the concepts examined in this section.

Demonstrating a common use of the radial menu, the `Chapter10-OptionWheel` example presents a scene where a player must confront a door and has multiple skills based on their in-game statistics. The outcomes for each option are represented by the name of the statistic:

Example 12 (InkOptionWheel.ink):

```
*   [Strength]
      You kick the door down.
*   [Intelligence]
      With a careful touch to two places where the wood has
         rotted, the door falls flat.
*   [Wisdom]
      You reach over and turn the knob. The door opens.
*   [Charisma]
      You turn to your companions and nod towards the door. One
         of them opens it for you.
```

In the code for *Example 12*, there are four options, each with the name of an example game statistic. When arranged in a simplified *radial* pattern, they might appear as the following in Unity:

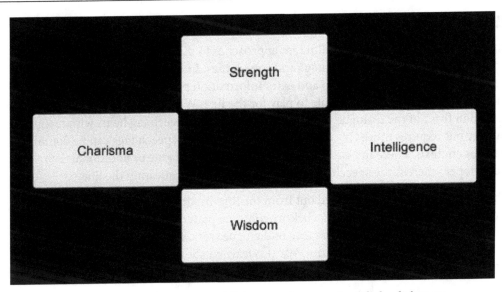

Figure 10.4 – The arrangement of dialogue options as a simplified radial menu

The **radial menu pattern** comes with the built-in limitation of reduced visual space. As mentioned in the *Listing dialogue options* section, the visual space given to the presentation of the options dictates how the information is presented. For the radial menu model, this is even more true.

As with the code for *Example 12*, the options presented on the screen must be matched to either the in-game statistics or the known outcomes to the player. For example, a player might know that if they select a certain icon, it will match a certain action. In these scenarios, they will be limited to no words in Ink to represent the option, with Unity taking more of the load to represent the option to the player as part of the user interface.

In this section, we reviewed the radial menu pattern. Presenting options in a clockwise arrangement, this pattern most often appears as part of a dialogue system for video game consoles with controllers or as part of a visual design with limited visual space. However, the use of the pattern has a direct effect on how options are written in ink. In one pattern, that is, lists, longer sentences can be included, but a player might not see all of them at once. For the other model, that is, the radial menu pattern, the options are only single words or perhaps even icons that represent more complex reactions.

Summary

In this chapter, we explored three different approaches to dialogue systems. In the first approach, we worked through hashtags and speech tags. In ink, we can add a hashtag to the end of a line. This allows you to add extra information per line such as the speaker for a line of dialogue or which media file to play for the line. With speech tags, a colon (:) can be added in front of the dialogue to mark the speaker. The speech tag helps with testing with Inky but requires more C# code in Unity. Hashtags and speech tags can be combined in various contexts where the hashtag can represent the media file or additional data for the developer whereas the speech tag contains who is communicating the line.

In the second approach, we zoomed out from the line-by-line emphasis with tags to the structures within ink. To replicate a click-to-continue pattern, we can combine a knot and the use of tunnels in ink. This is also true of dialogue trees, which we can break out into their own stitches within a larger knot. We also learned about the use of the CHOICE_COUNT() ink function and how to progress through a set of options.

In the final approach, we zoomed out from ink to consider visual designs in Unity and how they affect the writing of dialogue. The pattern used, whether a list or radial menu, will dictate how dialogue is created within ink. For a list, where each option can include multiple lines of text, a player will only see a limited selection at a time. For the radial menu pattern, where options are presented in a clockwise pattern on the screen, the dialogue within ink will be limited or nonexistent. In either case, the visual space for user interface elements directly affects how options are presented to a player.

In *Chapter 11*, *Quest Tracking and Branching Narratives*, we will move from smaller dialogue systems to the much larger ones of quest tracking and creating branching narratives. While many video games often present dialogue to a player, some track multiple values over longer periods. We will examine how the LIST ink keyword can be used to track quest progression and how larger ink projects can be broken up across multiple files for easier asset maintenance.

Questions

1. What is a hashtag in ink?
2. What are the differences between a hashtag and a speech tag?
3. How did the term *dialogue tree* get its name?
4. What is a list pattern?
5. What is a radial menu pattern?

11

Quest Tracking and Branching Narratives

In this chapter, we will review how to create an ink template for quests, track multiple quests based on this template, and show the player the values of variables across quests. In the first section, we will create an ink template and its required sections. Next, we will improve the ink template and create a `Quest` class to track multiple quests progressing independently from each other. Finally, we will show the player the results of progressing quests and view the values of change during this progression.

Many larger or narrative-focused video games are composed of separate quests for the player to complete. This chapter will provide a template for creating quests in ink and will also show you how to access and manipulate this template in Unity. Using multiple quests, a branching narrative approach is possible by allowing a player to progress through each quest separately, as explained in this chapter.

In this chapter, we will cover the following topics:

- Making a quest count
- Tracking progress across multiple quests
- Displaying and awarding player progression

> **Important**
>
> Each topic in this chapter has a separate, completed Unity project. Each topic includes instructions that state the name of the project and where to find it.

Technical requirements

The examples in this chapter have been divided into folders per project and can be found online on GitHub: `https://github.com/PacktPublishing/Dynamic-Story-Scripting-with-the-ink-Scripting-Language/tree/main/Chapter11`.

Making a quest count

In narrative terms, a **quest** is a series of events connected to a character within a story. In video games, quests are a sequence of connected events experienced by the *player*. In role-playing games, a quest might include unlocking a weapon, rescuing a prince, or defeating some great evil. Each point along the way is a *step* of the quest. Translated in terms of story and code, a quest can be thought of as a series of steps where the resolution of each step unlocks the next.

ink supports this pattern of smaller parts within a larger whole as stitches within a knot. Thought of in this way, each step of the quest can become its own stitch within the code, with the outcome of each stitch being able to move to the next within the larger structure. Using LIST in ink also allows us to define the steps we want by name, with a special knot progressing the player from one stitch to the next within the quest structure.

In this section, we will learn how to design a quest template in ink and access its values in Unity across one single project, with each section building on the previous one:

- In the first section, *Creating a quest template in ink*, we will review how to use this pattern and the built-in automation available by using existing Ink functions.

- In the second section, *Choosing specific knots in Unity*, we will move away from ink and look at Unity. Here, we will examine how to run the template in ink, as well as some potential issues to be aware of when using certain Story API methods.

> **Reminder**
>
> The completed project for this section can be found in the *Chapter 11*, examples on GitHub folder, under the name `Chapter11,QuestProgression`. Only select parts of the code will be shown as they relate to the concepts examined in the sections of this topic.

Now let us understand the next topic where we will create a quest template.

Creating a quest template in ink

ink stories are composed of different sections. In *Chapter 1*, *Text Flow, Choices, and Weaves*, we learned how ink breaks code into different sections called **knots**. Inside these, subsections can be defined called **stitches**. In *Chapter 2*, *Knots, Diverts, and Looping Patterns*, the concept of **diverts** was introduced, which are used to move between knots and their stitches. By putting these ideas together while using variables that use the VAR and LIST keywords in ink, which we did in *Chapter 4*, *Variables, Lists, and Functions*, we can create a quest that's composed of a series of steps:

```
LIST stages = (one), (two), (three)
VAR stage = one
VAR end = false
```

This code creates a list named `steps`, a variable named `step`, and a variable named `end` in ink. These three values keep track of the *quest's progression*. The name of each step in the quest is added as an entry to the list, with the first used as the value of the `stage` variable:

```
You meet an old man by the side of a dusty road with a wide hat
set out in front of him. "Got any change?"
* [Sure]
    -> quest
* [Not today]
    -> quest.stop
```

The player is presented with their first options: Sure and Not today. If the first is selected, the flow moves into the quest knot. If the second is selected, the flow moves to a stitch inside of the quest knot named stop:

```
== quest
{step:
    - one: -> first
    - two: -> second
    - three: -> third
}
-> DONE
```

The names *quest* and *stop* were chosen specifically. The use of the word *quest* helps in understanding the code as part of a template for other quests. As will be outlined in the next section, *Tracking progress across multiple quests*, multiple Story objects can exist at the same time in Unity. In this case, the word is used to show the pattern.

The quest knot contains the central logic of this pattern. Because the entries in a LIST in ink are Boolean values (either true or false), a multi-line comparison is used, where the order is important. The list named steps contains three entries, each of which are initially set to true. When the quest knot is first encountered, it will move the flow to the stitch named first:

```
= first
You empty some coins from your pocket and the old man nods.
"Thanks, stranger! May the gods bless you!"
-> DONE
```

The first stitch contains an unusual ending. The use of the DONE keyword usually signals that the story is over in ink. However, in this case, the DONE keyword is used to signal that the *step* is done. Instead of diverting to the quest knot or another section, the story seemingly stops. Progression happens using a combination of the LIST_MIN() function and the subtraction (-) operation for lists in Ink:

```
== progress
~ steps -= LIST_MIN(steps)
~ step = LIST_MIN(steps)
-> quest
```

Within the `progress` knot, each entry is removed (subtracted) and the top (minimum) value is used as part of the `step` variable. Each use of this knot *progresses* the quest by removing a step from the list and then using the top remaining one each time. However, the knot itself is not accessed directly. Instead, it is used externally by Unity.

In this section, we learned how each step can be divided into stitches as part of a knot named `quest`. By using a `LIST` and different variables in ink, progress can be tracked across the quest. In the next section, we will learn how an ink template can be used as a series of steps to access the `progress` knot externally in Unity.

Choosing specific knots in Unity

Different methods and properties of the Story API provided by the ink-Unity Integration plugin were covered in *Chapter 7, Unity API – Making Choices and Story Progression*, and *Chapter 8, Story API – Accessing ink Variables and Functions*. However, what was not covered in those chapters was a useful but potentially very dangerous method named `ChoosePathString()`. In this section, we will look at an example of how this method can be used safely.

Internally, the ink runtime uses the term "path string" to describe any knot that is part of a story. When loaded, these can be accessed by using the `ChoosePathString()` method, which forcibly moves the story to that section. In most cases, this is unwanted behavior, as its use will disregard any existing tunnels or threads. It can be thought of as *ripping* the flow away from wherever it was and dropping it into a new location.

As part of the ink runtime, variables are global. This means that while their values might be changed as part of the flow of a story, they exist outside of it. The values of variables are maintained despite any uses of the `ChoosePathString()` method. In other words, by carefully avoiding any structures that might be disrupted by its use, the `ChoosePathString()` method can be carefully used in projects.

In the previous section, the ink `progress` knot was introduced. To choose this path string in Unity using the `ChoosePathString()` method, only its name is needed:

```
public void Progress()
{
    InkStory.ChoosePathString("progress");
    FlipProgress();
    UpdateContent();
}
```

When the `ChoosePathString()` method is used with the `progress` ink knot, it *does* disrupt the flow of the story that's kept within the `InkStory` C# variable. However, as we learned, the values of variables are maintained throughout the story because of their global nature. The use of the `progress` ink knot *progresses* the quest to its next step by updating the variables each time.

The code also includes calls to two other methods: `FlipProgress()` and `UpdateContent()`. The first method sets a `Button` game object in Unity to inactive by using the `SetActive()` method in Unity. When a game object is turned off (set to inactive) in Unity, it does not appear on the screen. This code effectively sets the game object to appear as needed and to disappear when the player is selecting dialogue options:

```csharp
void FlipProgress() {
ProgressButton.gameObject.SetActive(!ProgressButton.gameObject.
activeSelf);

}
```

The second method, `UpdateContent()`, follows the pattern we first introduced in *Chapter 7, Unity API – Making Choices and Story Progression*, where a `Prefab` is used to dynamically create `Button` game objects as needed:

```csharp
void UpdateContent()
{

    DestroyChildren(OptionsPanel.transform);
    DialogueText.text = InkStory.ContinueMaximally();


    foreach (Choice in InkStory.currentChoices)
    {

        Button choiceButton = Instantiate(ButtonPrefab,
            OptionsPanel.transform);
        choiceButton.onClick.AddListener(delegate
        {

            InkStory.ChooseChoiceIndex(choice.index);
            FlipProgress();
            UpdateContent();
        });


        Text choiceText =
        choiceButton.GetComponentInChildren<Text>();
```

```
            choiceText.text = choice.text;
    }
}
```

In this section, we learned how to create a template for quests in ink. Using a knot and then individual stitches for each step, the parts were divided into different sections. Next, we looked at the `progress` ink knot. After that, we looked at Unity and using the `ChoosePathString()` method. While it can be potentially dangerous with larger projects using more advanced techniques, using variables in the ink quest template helped maintain their values. Finally, at the end of this section, the `ChoosePathString()` method in Unity was paired with the `progress` knot in ink. By using this knot, the Unity code could *progress* the quest, with ink updating its internal variables.

In the next section, we will continue with the pattern we looked at in this section by extending part of the quest template in ink and creating `Quest` and `Dialogue` classes in C#. These will allow us to track multiple quests at the same time.

Tracking progress across multiple quests

In the previous section, we created an ink template for a quest and then moved into Unity to create the user interface to progress the quest using the `ChoosePathString()` method. This forced the flow within ink to move to a specific location. In this section, we move beyond a single quest and start tracking multiple quests at the same time. To do this, the ink template needs additional variables. For this, we will need the `Quest` and `Dialogue` classes in C#. We also will depart from using a single ink file and start using multiple files. For every quest, we will create a separate file and use the `Quest` class to track the progress of each in Unity with the `Dialogue` class, which handles creating options for a player to choose from during each step in the quest.

First, we will update the ink template with a new variable we will access later in Unity. Then, we will create the `Quest` and `Dialogue` classes in Unity. After that, we will access multiple ink files in Unity to present an interface containing multiple quests. Finally, we will allow a user to toggle between quests and progress them independently of each other.

> **Reminder**
> The completed project for this section can be found in the *Chapter 11 examples on GitHub* folder, under the name *Chapter11-MultipleQuests*. Only select parts of the code will be shown as they relate to the concepts examined in the sections of this topic.

Building on the ink quest template

As we saw in *Chapter 8, Story API – Accessing ink Variables and Functions*, we can access ink variables that have been created with the VAR keyword using the variablesState property in Unity. This allows us to retrieve the value of a variable based on its name. With that in mind, the existing ink template can be expanded to include a new variable for each quest – its name.

By understanding that the compiled ink files will be operated from Unity, we can anticipate certain needs we will have with quests. For example, a quest usually has a *name*. We can then define this variable alongside our existing values in Ink:

```
LIST steps = (one), (two), (three)
VAR step = one
VAR end = false


VAR name = "Old Man's Change"
```

Once we know that the name variable exists in ink, we can read it in Unity. However, unlike what was shown in the previously section, we will need to observe the end ink variable as well:

```
InkStory = new Story(text);
Name = (string)InkStory.variablesState["name"];
End = (bool)InkStory.variablesState["end"];


InkStory.ObserveVariable("end", delegate
{
        End = (bool)InkStory.variablesState["end"];
});
```

These small changes may not seem important, but by establishing a pattern where certain variables exist (name and end) and all files containing quests will also have a knot named progress (as defined in the previous section), we can write any quests we want if those parts remain the same.

Once these variables have been prepared, we can start creating the Quest and Dialogue classes, which will hold the values we defined in ink and read them in Unity.

Making Quest and Dialogue classes in Unity

In the previous section, we combined a simple presentation of dialogue options with the values and methods to progress the single quest presented. In this section, we will break that functionality into two new classes in Unity: `Quest` and `Dialogue`.

Most of the `Quest` class was shown in the previous section. However, its purpose is to hold a `Story` object and to expose a method named `Progress()` that internally calls the `ChoosePathString()` method:

```
using Ink.Runtime;

public class Quest
{
    public Story InkStory;
    public string Name;
    public string Description;
    public bool End;

    public Quest(string text)
    {
        InkStory = new Story(text);
        Name = (string)InkStory.variablesState["name"];
        End = (bool)InkStory.variablesState["end"];

        InkStory.ObserveVariable("end", delegate
        {
            End = (bool)InkStory.variablesState["end"];
        });
    }
    public void Progress()
    {
        InkStory.ChoosePathString("progress");
    }
}
```

The `Quest` class is small because it is used by other classes. Its sole purpose is to contain the quest (ink story) and provide a way to progress the quest (via the `Progress()` method).

The new class, `Dialogue`, performs most of the work to create the `Button` game objects needed and to remember what the last line of dialogue was as a reminder for the player. Its `UpdateContent()` method looks like the example code that was first shown in *Chapter 7, Unity API – Making Choices and Story Progression*, except for using the new `Quest` class:

```
public void UpdateContent()
{
    DestroyChildren();

    if(quest.InkStory.canContinue)
    {
        DialogueText.text =
            quest.InkStory.ContinueMaximally();
        lastDialogue = DialogueText.text;
    }
    else
    {
        DialogueText.text = lastDialogue;
    }
```

With the updated ink template from the first section and the introduction of the `Quest` and `Dialogue` classes in this section, two more parts are needed:

- Quests need to be based on compiled JSON files
- Players need to be able to toggle which quest they are progressing

In the next section, we will start with the first part by learning how to read files and creating a new `Quest` class per file found.

Organizing multiple quest files

In the previous examples in this book, a single ink file was used per project. This section will break away from that pattern. To track multiple quests, we will define each quest in its own file and then read the compiled JSON files. The `Quest` class, which we looked at in the previous section, will hold the contents and expose some of the values in each file. The `Dialogue` class will create the options the player will see based on the `Quest` class's values. First, however, we will need to read the files.

This book follows the recommended naming convention of Unity folders and has placed all the Ink files in a folder named Ink. Using the **Compile All Ink Automatically** option in the **Project Settings** window, each created ink file will also contain a JSON file:

Figure 11.1 – Compiled JSON files in the Ink folder

Because Unity can run on many different operating systems, it exposes the Assets folder (shown in the **Project** window) as part of a global property named Application. dataPath. This is the *path* to the data, as part of the currently running application. Based on this value, any additional folders can be found, and their files can be accessed:

```
void GetFiles()
{
    string inkPath = Application.dataPath + "/Ink/";
    foreach(string file in Directory.GetFiles(inkPath,
        "*.json"))
    {
        string contents = File.ReadAllText(file);
        quests.Add(new Quest(contents));
    }
}
```

By using the Application.dataPath property, each compiled ink file (JSON file) can be read, and a new object based on the Quest class is created. This not only allows each quest to operate independently of each other via their quest progression, but it also exposes values that the Dialogue class can use to present different options to the player.

In the next and final section, we will write some code that will allow a player to toggle between which quest is active for them and see the Quest and Dialogue classes in action.

Toggling quests

In Unity, the `Toggle` game object allows a user to select a single item among a group of items. For its usage in the project that's part of this section, a `Toggle` prefab must be created. Like the usage of `Button` game objects, these are created as needed. As each `Toggle` game object is based on an object using the `Quest` class, this means the `GetFiles()` method (shown in the previous section, *Organizing multiple quest files*) is run first, and the resulting quests are used to make the `Toggle` game objects:

```
void CreateQuestToggles()
{
    foreach(Quest q in quests)
    {
        Toggle questToggle = Instantiate(QuestTogglePrefab,
            QuestPanel.transform);
        questToggle.group =QuestPanel.GetComponent
            <ToggleGroup>();

        Text questToggleText = questToggle
            .GetComponentInChildren<Text>();
        questToggleText.text = q.Name;
    }
}
```

The `CreateQuestToggles()` method references a component named `ToggleScript`. This is a `Script` component that is part of each `Toggle` prefab. Each time one is created, its values are set:

```
ToggleScript ts = questToggle.GetComponent<ToggleScript>();
ts.quest = q;
ts.DialogueText = DialogueText;
ts.ButtonPrefab = ButtonPrefab;
ts.OptionsPanel = OptionsPanel;
ts.ProgressPanel = ProgressPanel;
ts.ProgressButtonPrefab = ProgressButtonPrefab;
```

This process, starting with the GetFiles() method, creates objects based on the Quest class first. Next, Toggle prefabs are created, and values are passed to its Script component. Internally, the Toggle prefab creates an additional Script component based on the Dialogue class:

```
dialogue = gameObject.AddComponent<Dialogue>();
dialogue.quest = quest;
dialogue.DialogueText = DialogueText;
dialogue.ButtonPrefab = ButtonPrefab;
dialogue.OptionsPanel = OptionsPanel;
```

The reason for this multiple-step process of creating objects based on the Quest class, and then leading to the Dialogue class, is to allow each Toggle prefab to control what is shown to the player:

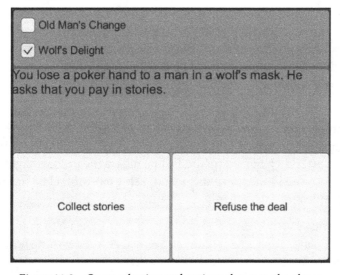

Figure 11.2 – Quest selection and options shown to the player

Upon clicking on a Toggle prefab, its object is enabled based on the Dialogue class, showing the current text and options to the player. These, in turn, are based on the Quest class's values, as passed to the Dialogue class.

The combined effect of the code is to create separate quests. Depending on which is active, as determined by each Toggle prefab selected by the player, they will see different dialogue options and be presented with the ability to progress each quest independently of each other at the end of each step. This combines the ink template that we created in the first section with a multiple-quest approach, as shown in this section, which uses multiple files and adds the ability to progress across individual quests, independent of each other.

In the next section, we will examine how to award player progression by passing information between quests. This will build on the project we created for this section and the concepts from the first section.

Displaying and awarding player progression

In programming, there are two approaches to accessing values in one system from another: **polling** and **events-based**. Either a value can be checked if it has changed (*polling*) or one system can wait for a message (*event*) from the other to signal that a value has changed. Because the second system must wait for an event to happen, this is often known as the **observer pattern** because the second system is *observing* events.

In the first section, we saw an example of polling in action. Each time a step of the quest came to its end, the Unity code checked (*polled*) the ink values to see if it should show a Button game object and allow the player to progress the quest. The second section moved us closer to an events-based approach, where the ObserveVariable() method was used within the Quest class. In the second project, whenever the end ink variable changed, it updated the End property of the Quest class in Unity. As this value (the End property) was used as part of determining whether the quest could progress, this made the second project more dynamic than the one that was used in the first project.

To award a player for completing a quest or achieving some outcome as part of one quest in another, information needs to be passed between them. Because the ink runtime already supports an events-based approach via its ObserveVariable() and ObserveVariables() named methods, this makes the process slightly easier. However, as we introduced in the previous section, using a Quest class means each ink story is now independent of each other.

In this section, we will start by creating a way for each Quest class to share changes as they happen while a player is progressing them. We will end by learning how to show the player this information as they complete different quests.

> **Reminder**
>
> The completed project for this section can be found in the *Chapter 11 examples on GitHub* folder, under the name *Chapter11-TrackingQuests*. Only select parts of the code will be shown as they relate to the concepts examined in the sections of this topic.

Tracking quest values

The `Story` class method, `ObserveVariables()`, can track different variables based on their names. However, the existing ink template contains the variables it uses to track progression. This means that the first step of tracking quest values is to make a list of variables to exclude from tracking as part of an expanded `Quest` class:

```
public Story InkStory;
public string Name;
public string Description;
public bool End;
public List<string> excludeVariables = new List<string>(){
"step", "steps", "name", "end" };
```

Next, all the variables contained in the `variablesState` property, excluding those in the created list used to track quest progression, need to be tracked. This means that for each variable, it can be added to a separate list to be passed to the `Story` method known as `ObserveVariables()`. This can be part of the `ObserveVariables()` method, as part of the `Quest` method, so that it matches the one on the `Story` class:

```
public void ObserveVariables(Story.VariableObserver callback)
{
    List<string> variables = new List<string>();

    foreach(string n in InkStory.variablesState)
    {
        if(!excludeVariables.Contains(n))
        {
            variables.Add(n);
        }
    }

    InkStory.ObserveVariables(variables, callback);
}
```

The new `ObserveVariables()` method that was added to the `Quest` class accepts a single parameter, `Story.VariableObserver`. Internally, the `Story` class defines a `delegate` method called `VariableObserver`. Using the same type for the new method allows other methods to be passed through the `Quest` method to the `Story` method of the same name. In other words, the new method works the same as the existing one, but it will exclude a specific list of variable names.

While observing variables, there also needs to be a way to update the values of variables across all quests whenever a value changes in one. Using the existing `variablesState` property, a new method can be added to the `Quest` class named `UpdateVariable()`:

```
public void UpdateVariable(string name, object value)
{
        if(InkStory.variablesState.GlobalVariableExistsWith
        Name(name))
    {
        if (!InkStory.variablesState[name].Equals(value))
        {
            InkStory.variablesState[name] = value;
        }
    }
}
```

Inside the `UpdateVariable()` method are two important checks. The first uses the `GlobalVariableExistsWithName()` method. This method checks if a variable exists. Without this check, if one quest added a variable another did not have, the entire project could crash. The second check verifies whether the variable to be updated does not already have the same value. Without this second check, updating a variable would trigger a variable change in any other quests, which would trigger another update. This would eventually cause a crash as quests would be trying to update each other in an endless loop.

Between the two new methods, `ObserveVariables()` and `UpdateVariable()`, one more part is needed: the two methods must be combined. Based on the project from the second section, *Tracking progress across multiple quests*, the `InkStoryScript` code is the best place to add this combination. The reason for this placement is because this will allow each quest to be configured as part of the existing loop:

```
foreach(Quest q in quests)
{
    q.ObserveVariables((name, value) =>
    {
```

```
            UpdateAllQuests(name, value);
    });
}
```

This new code references an additional method, `UpdateAllQuests()`. When passed the name of a variable and its value, this new method works through the existing quests and updates their values by calling `UpdateVariable()` per quest:

```
void UpdateAllQuests(string name, object value)
{
    foreach (Quest q in quests)
    {
        q.UpdateVariable(name, value);
    }
}
```

In this section, we have defined multiple new methods. We added two to the `Quest` class called `ObserveVariables()` and `UpdateVariable()`. These detect changes using the event approach. ink will signal to Unity when a variable in one of the quests changes. We also added code to `InkStoryScript` by using a new method called `UpdateAllQuests()`, which will update the same variable in other quests.

In the next section, we will finalize this project. Detecting changes and updating other quests help keep all of them updated as changes happen. Next, we need to show data to the player as changes happen.

Showing player progress

In the previous section, we created the necessary code to keep all the variables used across quests updated. To show the player this data, we must add a new game object named `StatisticsText`. Next, we need to use a special keyword in C#: `static`.

Any method or property using the `static` keyword in C# exists outside of any instances of the class. This means that the property can be accessed or the method can be called anywhere in the project. However, this comes with a major caveat: any `static` method can only access `static` properties. To allow another class (`Dialogue`) to be able to call a `static` method in `InkStoryScript` (which holds all the quests), the existing quests and new `StatisticsText` variable must both use the `static` keyword:

```
public GameObject QuestPanel;
public Toggle QuestTogglePrefab;
```

```
public Text DialogueText;
public Button ButtonPrefab;
public GameObject OptionsPanel;
public GameObject ProgressPanel;
public Button ProgressButtonPrefab;
public static GameObject StatisticsText;
static List<Quest> quests;
```

With the quests and StatisticsText properties, they can be accessed by a new method named ShowStatistics():

```
public static void ShowStatistics()
{
    StatisticsText =
      GameObject.Find("/Canvas/Right/StatisticsText");
    Dictionary<string, object> vars = new
      Dictionary<string, object>();

    foreach (Quest q in quests)
    {
        foreach(string s in q.InkStory.variablesState)
        {
            if(!vars.ContainsKey(s) &&
              !q.excludeVariables.Contains(s))
            {
                vars.Add(s,
                  q.InkStory.variablesState[s]);
            }
        }
    }

    Text stats = StatisticsText.GetComponent<Text>();
    stats.text = "";

    foreach (KeyValuePair<string, object> entry in vars)
    {
        stats.text += entry.Key + ": " + entry.Value +
```

```
        "\n";
    }
}
```

The new `ShowStatistics()` method uses a `Dictionary<string, object>`. This combines the name of the variable (`string`) with its value (`object`). However, a `Dictionary` in C# comes with an obstacle: it can only contain unique keys. In the `ShowStatistics()` method, the use of the `ContainsKey()` method prevents this issue.

To set up a method that can be called by another class, the new `ShowStatistics()` code must be placed within the `Dialogue` class as part of its `UpdateContent()` method, after the creation of the `Button` game objects based on the current choices:

```
foreach (Choice in quest.InkStory.currentChoices)
{
    Button choiceButton = Instantiate(ButtonPrefab,
        OptionsPanel.transform);
    choiceButton.onClick.AddListener(delegate
    {
        quest.InkStory.ChooseChoiceIndex(choice.index);
        UpdateContent();
    });

    Text choiceText =
        choiceButton.GetComponentInChildren<Text>();
    choiceText.text = choice.text;
}


InkStoryScript.ShowStatistics();
```

The new code will always show the latest values of the variables as the values are updated. Because each quest handles updating its variables based on an event-based approach, any user action for making choices or selecting a quest will update all the values being tracked by the project and constantly show player progression.

In this section, we awarded player progression by showing the player's the updated values. We started by adding some code from the previous section to constantly update the variables with the same names across all quests. This keeps all the quests connected. Then, we created a `ShowStatistics()` method to show these values and updated a `Text` game object with their names and values.

Summary

We started this chapter by creating an ink template. By defining variables and a `progress` knot in ink, we can move through the various sections of a quest as individual stitches within a larger knot. Next, we looked at the `ChoosePathString()` method, which can forcibly move a story to a new section.

In the second section, we broke away from single files and developed a `Quest` class. Each object based on the `Quest` class contained an ink `Story` object based on different files and a method named `Progress()`, which calls the `ChoosePathString()` method internally. As part of this section, we learned how the `Quest` and `Dialogue` classes can help organize functionality into different classes.

Finally, we displayed the name and values of variables. First, we added new methods to detect variable changes in any quest using an events-based approach. This triggered other variables with the same name in other quests to have their values updated. Then, we added the `ShowStatistics()` method to display these updating values.

In the next chapter, *Chapter 12, Procedural Storytelling with ink*, we will review the basics of procedurally organizing different story sections and content. While looking at two approaches, either coding values in ink or loading data into ink dynamically, we will examine when one approach might be better, depending on the context.

Q&A

1. What is a quest?
2. What is the name of the knot that's used to progress a quest based on the ink template shown in this chapter?
3. How does the `ChoosePathString()` method work?
4. What is the name of the global property where Unity records the path for the data of the application?
5. What is the difference between polling and events-based approaches?

12
Procedural Storytelling with ink

In this chapter, we will review **procedural storytelling** using ink and Unity. Inkle, the company that created and maintains the narrative scripting language ink, has published multiple games that combine ink and Unity. These games use procedural storytelling to provide different experiences per session based on randomness and player choices. This chapter will introduce approaches to achieving this same general result: loading values in ink and coding collections in Unity.

In the first topic, we will review the term *procedural storytelling* more generally. Based on concepts initially introduced in *Chapter 3, Sequences, Cycles, and Shuffling Text*, we will learn how to use a shuffle in ink to create dynamic content based on simple rules.

Diving even deeper into ink, the second topic will demonstrate how to load values in ink. This process focuses on using ink to generate content for players based on simple rules.

In the final topic, we will switch the emphasis from ink to Unity. We will use Unity to load values and call functions in ink to process values instead. This approach uses more complex code in Unity, but simpler code in ink.

In this chapter, we will cover the following topics:

- Introducing procedural storytelling in ink
- Loading values into ink
- Coding collections in Unity

Technical requirements

The examples in this chapter can be found online on GitHub: `https://github.com/PacktPublishing/Dynamic-Story-Scripting-with-the-ink-Scripting-Language/tree/main/Chapter12`.

Introducing procedural storytelling in ink

The term *procedural storytelling* takes its name from another term, *procedural generation*. The word "procedural" preceding "generation" means that content is created based on a sequence of *procedures*; that is, rules. When referring to generating assets such as 3D models or placing non-player characters within some world in a video game, the term *procedural generation* applies. When discussing planning, generating, or dynamically ordering content related to the story or experienced narrative of the player within an interactive project, the better term to use is **procedural storytelling**.

Procedural storytelling occurs when a project uses rules to define how a player may interact with or encounter parts of its story content. For example, if a project has a set of rules to create dynamic names for its characters, a player in a science fiction setting may interact with a generated character name of *Neldronor*, while a different player might see the name *Vynear* for the same entity. Procedurally generating story content can also extend beyond substituting names to deciding which quests a player may have access to, when they encounter certain characters, or even the possible events that may happen in their play session.

In this topic, we will cover three examples of simple patterns for understanding procedural generation in ink based on randomness. The first, *Random encounters*, will explain how to combine the use of a shuffle and threads in ink to create a listing of possible encounters for a player. The second pattern, *Weighted randomness*, uses the same concepts as the first pattern but defines the weighted probability a player might see some content. Both patterns are easy ways to add simple procedural generation to an existing project without too much disruption to its existing structure. The last section and pattern, *Conditional content*, will cover using the previous actions and input from a player to influence which encounter a player sees. It does so by using concepts from the two previous patterns.

Random encounters

Many tabletop role-playing games use a concept known as a **random table**. In the material or book for the game, there is a table or list of possible things a player might encounter in a location or scene. The person running the game would roll some dice, consult the table to find the row matching the rolled number, and then tell the players what they encountered. This system creates the possibility for *random* encounters. Based on the random element of the dice, the player would see or interact with different things each time they used the same table to generate content for their game.

Translated into a digital setting, the random tables of tabletop games can become a set of possible encounters. In ink, we can create this using a shuffle and threads:

```
{shuffle:
    - <- encounter.animal
    - <- encounter.machine
    - <- encounter.person
}
```

Because the shuffle will always pick one of its entries at random, each thread has the same probability of occurring. However, as is perhaps not as obvious, *each possible encounter is additional content.* Unlike a much more authored experience without any procedural storytelling functionality, even a simple addition such as a table of possible encounters means creating new content per possible encounter:

Example 1:

```
{shuffle:
    - <- encounter.animal
    - <- encounter.machine
    - <- encounter.person
}
== encounter
= animal
You hear a soft thud and then see a face peering at you. The
sound starts as if it is a meow and then turns into language
the longer you listen. "Meee-Hello. Sorry. I'm not used to
talking to people.
-> DONE
= machine
The small machine buzzes to life in front of you. "Hi, there!
```

```
I'm Ge8at10, but you can call me 'Great!'"
-> DONE

= person
You look around and see a man standing awkwardly against a
tree. He waves and then looks away before speaking. "Uh. Yeah.
Over here. Hi."
-> DONE
```

Example 1 demonstrates using a shuffle in ink containing three different threads as a simple random encounter system. Each thread references a knot called `encounter` with a stitch named after the kind of encounter, such as `animal`. Based on random selection, the player would see one of three possible encounters.

Using random encounters, as defined within a shuffle, is an easy way to add simple procedural storytelling in ink to a project. It does require adding extra content per entry in the shuffle, but such a pattern can be the least disruptive to an existing project. It is also possible to have additional sets and create more dynamic outcomes where a player might encounter any number of things across multiple settings, contexts, or levels where each usage is based on a shuffle and threads in ink.

In the next section, we will examine weighted probabilities as part of controlling the randomness of a set of encounters. Instead of all entries having an equal probability of occurring, as is the case when using a shuffle, there may be situations where certain encounters should occur more often for players.

Weighted randomness

The shuffle is powerful functionality in ink. It allows us to create a set of possible entries and then randomly select one. As was seen in the *Random encounters* section, a simple set of possible encounters can be created; then, a shuffle can be used to select one as needed.

However, there may be situations where equally weighted probabilities are not wanted. For example, a developer may only want a player to encounter a character 30% of the time when traveling through a forest area in a game. For these situations, we want to *weight* the randomness of encounters.

In ink, the RANDOM() function allows us to define the range of random whole numbers that are produced. If we wanted numbers between 1 and 10, we could use RANDOM(1,10). Based on the number that's returned by the RANDOM() function, it is possible to test values and only act if its result is in a certain range:

Example 2:

```
VAR percentage = 0
~ percentage = RANDOM(1,10)
{
    - percentage <= 3:
        <- encounter.brown_wizard
    - else:
        <- encounter.travel
}
== encounter
= brown_wizard
As you move through the forest, you encounter a strange man on
a sled driven by large rabbits. You talk for a moment before
the man moves away from you and deeper into the forest.
-> DONE
= travel
They travel through the forest.
-> DONE
```

In *Example 2*, the brown_wizard stitch is only encountered if the result from the use of RANDOM(1, 10) is less than or equal to 3. This creates a 30% chance of the player encountering this character. This is an example of a *weighted* probability. Instead of an equal probability between the two encounters, one is weighted more than the other. The travel stitch is more likely to be encountered by the player than the other stitch, brown_wizard.

In the previous section, *Random encounters*, we learned how to create different content within stitches and select them with equal probability using a shuffle. In this section, we controlled this randomness using a weighted probability with the RANDOM() function in ink.

In the next section, we will combine this and the previous pattern for *conditional* content. Based on the previous options that were selected by a player, we can influence what the player encounters using both randomness and by comparing other values.

Conditional content

In projects that don't use randomness, it is very common to use conditional blocks or choices to respond to what the player selects and how they are progressing through a story. As we saw in the *Random encounters* and *Weighted randomness* sections, we can also use shuffles and the RANDOM() function in ink to shape a story. In this section, we will look at an example of using both concepts together to create more complex procedures to generate connections between content for players.

In the previous section, *Weighted randomness*, we saw how we can create a set of different conditional statements within a block to control what the player encounters next. In *Example 2*, this was the weighted outcomes of either the brown_wizard or travel stitch, with the travel stitch more likely to be seen by the player. However, players rarely want to only read the text in a game. They want to have some input over what happens as part of a story.

By using labels with choices in ink, we can test whether a player selects a particular option and then influence the weighted outcome for the player:

Example 3:

```
VAR percentage = 0
A vast forest stretches out before you and alongside the forest
is a winding river.
* (travel_forest) [Enter the forest]
* (travel_river) [Travel by river]
-
~ percentage = RANDOM(1,10)
{
    - percentage <= 3 && travel_forest == 1:
        <- encounter.brown_wizard
    - percentage > 3 && travel_forest == 1:
        <- encounter.travel
    - travel_river == 1:
        <- encounter.river
}
== encounter
= brown_wizard
As you move through the forest, you encounter a strange man on
a sled driven by large rabbits. You talk for a moment before
```

```
the man moves away from you and deeper into the forest.
-> DONE
= travel
They travel through the forest.
-> DONE
= river
You travel down the river safely.
-> DONE
```

Example 3 is an updated form of *Example 2*. However, instead of merely showing text, the player is presented with two options within a weave. Depending on which one they select, the story then branches along two possible paths. In the first, if the player chooses to travel in the forest, there is a 30% chance they will encounter a character. In the second, if a player chooses to travel by the river, they will not encounter the character.

While some projects might use shuffle or weighted options, many more incorporate player selections and past choices with randomness. This not only gives the player more control over what they are experiencing, but it also allows the author to craft a story, along with certain predictable outcomes. Instead of trying to account for multiple outcomes when only using a shuffle, the use of the weave and its limited number of options shapes the possible paths of future encounters. Because there are only two options in the wave, there are only two possible main branches, with the weighted randomness only affecting one and not the other.

In this topic, we have examined three different patterns for introducing or adjusting simple procedural storytelling rules in ink projects. In the first section, *Random encounters*, we learned how to create a set of equally weighted entries using a shuffle with threads to pull in different story content. In the second section, *Weighted randomness*, we explored how to control randomness with weighted outcomes where one outcome was more likely than another.

In the last section, *Conditional content*, we combined randomness with the result of players selecting options and investigated how to create seemingly more advanced rules, where the number of choices within a weave has a stronger influence on the shape of the story than the randomness contained within any one branch.

In the next topic, we will look at more complex patterns. For many projects, ink will be the driving force behind content generation and how the project uses procedural storytelling. We will look at how to load values into ink as part of examining how to write a grammar for stories, and then plan how players will encounter its different parts in dynamic ways.

Loading values into ink

The *procedural* aspect of procedural storytelling can exist either primarily in ink or Unity. In this topic, we will examine the process of loading values into ink. We will center a design focused on letting ink make procedural decisions about what content a user might see or interact with during a play session.

In the first section, *Substitution grammars*, we will consider how to use what we learned in the previous section, *Introducing procedural storytelling in ink*, to build a set of possible events for a player. This will lead us into the next section, *Story planning*, where we will apply rules to the grammars themselves. This will allow us to control how different sets of encounters are influenced by previous ones, creating simple formulas for complex stories.

Substitution grammars

In linguistics, **grammar** describes the rules that define how a language works. For example, in English, there is a specific order of subject, verb, and object in sentences. In programming contexts, we can define what is called **substitution grammar**, where a set of rules describes how words or phrases are replaced with others. This can often be used to define a specific order, such as the use of subjects and verbs in an English sentence. In a programming context, dynamic constructions can be produced where dynamic or random values are *substituted* in specific places in the defined pattern.

In ink, we can create functions to return values based on shuffles. By writing a grammar – that is, rules for what order entries appear in – we can create a simple substitution pattern where random entries are used from specific sets to create a dynamic text interaction:

Example 4:

```
First, we saw the {getLocation()}. Next, we visited the
    {getMarker()}.
== function getLocation() ==
~ return "{~tower|ruin|temple}"
== function getMarker() ==
~ return "{~grave|farmstead|ancient tree}"
```

In *Example 4*, the getLocation() and getMarker() ink functions provide the substitutions within the grammar of the sentence. By placing shuffles within the functions and surrounding them with quotation marks, the text's result can be returned; that is, where the functions are called. Because all functions are global, this also means they can be used multiple times in the code.

> **Warning**
>
> Based on *Example 4*, it can be tempting to assume functions can also be used to generate possible divert targets using a shuffle. This is not the case. While variables can hold divert targets, functions are not allowed to divert in ink, and the language prevents combinations of calling functions and using the returned value to thread or divert to another section in a story.

Functions in ink can be useful for generating and returning text. However, because of its design, ink does not allow functions to control story flow. In cases where each entry within a shuffle might also want to use diverting or threads, we can create an extended tunnel where each part of the tunnel acts as part of the grammar:

Example 5:

```
location -> marker -> DONE

== location
First, we saw the <>
{shuffle:
    - tower
    - ruin
    - temple
}<>.
->->

== marker
Next, we saw the <>
{shuffle:
    - grave
    - farmstead
    - ancient tree
}<>.
->->
```

Example 5 is a rewritten version of *Example 4* using an extended tunnel. For simple text substitution, the pattern shown in *Example 4*, which is using shuffles and functions, can be very useful. However, the pattern in *Example 5*, which is using knots and multi-line shuffles, allows each entry in the shuffle to potentially divert or use threads themselves. This is often the preferred pattern for creating a substitution grammar, where each part of the grammar can expand as needed.

In this section, we learned how to use substitution grammar for text and then a more advanced one for incorporating tunnels. In the next section, we will apply substitution grammar as part of a planning process for stories. Loops and other conditional aspects will be introduced to create more advanced substitution grammars.

Story planning

In the previous section, we saw how substitution grammars can provide us with a specific order of events. By using shuffles, we can pick random entries for each part and create a dynamic experience for a player. In the examples shown in the previous section, there was also only one entry per part of the grammar. There was one for `location`, one for `marker`, and then the tunnel ended. This is useful, but many games will want to create dynamic patterns based on previous entries. In other words, it is also possible to base the range of future entries on previous ones within a grammar.

When we create a formula where previous entries can affect future entries as part of advanced grammar, we are using a concept called **story planning**. In procedural storytelling, story planning occurs when the story is *planned* based on rules for generating more complex patterns than simple substitution.

As explained in *Chapter 3*, *Sequences, Cycles, and Shuffling Text*, alternatives can be embedded inside each other. This means we can use alternatives inside of multi-line conditional blocks to create contexts where, based on previous values, random entries can be chosen:

Example 6:

```
VAR location_pick = 0

-> location -> marker -> DONE

== location
First, we saw the <>
{shuffle:
    - tower
```

```
            ~ location_pick = "tower"
        - ruin
            ~ location_pick = "ruin"
        - temple
            ~ location_pick = "temple"
}<>.
->->


== marker
Next, we saw the <>
{
    - location_pick == "tower":
        {shuffle:
            - grave
            - memorial stone
        }
    - else:
        {shuffle:
            - farmstead
            - ancient tree
        }
}<>.
->->
```

In *Example 6*, a new variable has been introduced based on the code from *Example 5*. In this new version, the values of the marker knot are based on the location_pick variable. Within the extended tunnel moving from the location knot to the marker knot, the location_pick variable is changed. Depending on its value moving into the marker knot, different results can be produced. If the random entry from location is "tower", the first two values, grave and memorial stone, are enabled. Otherwise, the farmstead and ancient tree values are.

In this topic, we focused on loading and generating values in ink. In the first section, *Substitution grammars*, we learned how to create simple patterns. In this section, *Story planning*, we reviewed a simple example of story planning using a single variable for branching within the second part of a tunnel. Depending on the planning that's wanted, authors can create very complex grammars using different variables where previous values can branch out future calculations and ranges of entries in shuffles or other alternatives.

In the next topic, we will move away from ink and back into Unity. When it comes to scripting narrative experiences, ink is an incredible language. However, ink does not work well with more complex value manipulations. In Unity, with the use of C#, we can perform much more complicated procedural storytelling approaches, where we can make decisions about which ink story to load and how to pass its values to make decisions internally.

Coding collections in Unity

In the previous topic, we examined ways to have ink create and plan content for a player. In this section, we move back into Unity. Often, in large projects, story and otherwise, narrative content will be one of several complex interlocking mechanics in a game. In these cases, procedural storytelling will be one of multiple systems, and Unity, as the game engine driving the project, will be programmed to use one story over another as part of more complex operations and planning. In these cases, the narrative content is stored in what C# names *collections*. These can be something as simple as an array or a much more complex data structure capable of sorting its internal elements based on patterns or the values of their internal elements.

In the first section, *Using multiple stories*, we will look at an example of moving the procedural storytelling aspect of a project from ink into Unity. Instead of working with shuffles in ink, we will use randomness in Unity to select between different possible stories within a collection and then remove them from future selections. This will allow us to concentrate on the story content in ink, creating dialog or player choices within separate files, and then use Unity to choose what to show a player.

In the final section, *Conditionally choosing stories*, we will apply the concept of simple story planning, as shown in the *Story planning* subsection, using ink in Unity. Much like it did in ink, this will allow us to start to define a substitution grammar for how we want story content to appear to the player, but with the coded collections in Unity performing the work of selecting parts instead of ink.

Using multiple stories

As we first explored in *Chapter 11, Quest Tracking and Branching Narratives*, in the *Tracking progress across multiple quests* topic, it is possible to use multiple ink files as separate instances of the Story class in a project. In that topic, each file was a separate quest. However, it is also possible to use each file as a scene within a larger story. In these cases, each ink file would represent a separate narrative experience for a player. This could become part of a session or a longer story, upon being selected by Unity, to show the player in a random order.

> **Note**
>
> The completed project for this section can be found in the *Chapter 12* examples on GitHub under the name `Chapter12-MultipleStories`. Only select parts of the code will be shown as they relate to the concepts being examined.

When you're using multiple ink files to break a story down into different scenes where each could be accessed independently of each other, the easiest way to approach this is to load them all at once. The following project uses a method named `GetFiles()` to process the compiled JSON files and create `Story` class instances. With each new object that's created, it is added to a `List<Story>` collection named `Stories`:

```
void GetFiles()
{
        string inkPath = Application.dataPath + "/Ink/";
        foreach (string file in Directory.GetFiles(inkPath,
          "*.json"))
        {
                string contents = File.ReadAllText(file);
                Stories.Add(new Story(contents));
        }
}
```

In the *Random encounter* section of the *Introducing procedural storytelling in ink* topic, a shuffle was used to pick between different threads. In C#, the `Random` class works similarly. It provides random data based on some range. Using its `Next()` method and the `Count` property of the collection, it provides an index to select between entries in the `List<Story>` collection, which is populated by the `GetFiles()` method:

```
void PickRandomStory()
{
        if (Stories.Count > 0)
        {
                System.Random rand = new System.Random();
                int index = rand.Next(Stories.Count);
                Story entry = Stories[index];
                Stories.RemoveAt(index);
                UpdateContent(entry);
        }
```

```
    else
    {
            SceneDescription.text = "(There are no more
                stories.)";
    }
}
```

To prevent the same story from appearing again, the `RemoveAt()` method removes the entry from the `List<Story>` collection at random. This prevents the same story from being shown twice.

Put together, the `Start()` method is used to call multiple other methods to parse the files and pick a random story. Based on the weave contained in the randomly picked `Story`, a method named `UpdateContent()`, which is called from `PickRandomStory()`, presents two options to the player as `Button` game objects. Clicking on either of these changes the value of a variable within the story. This is then shown to the player as updates to two variables, `violence` and `peace`, which are tracked in Unity:

```
void Start()
{
    Stories = new List<Story>();
    UpdateStatistics();
    GetFiles();
    PickRandomStory();
}
```

While relatively simple, the project shown in this section illustrates an important aspect of balancing between ink and Unity as separate systems for procedural storytelling. The complexity of an ink story is not reflected in the C# code needed to pick it from a collection or show its contents. Simple code can be used in Unity to randomly select an ink story that, itself, uses randomness, substitution grammars, or its story planning in its design. In Unity, the C# `Random` class can be used without any knowledge of what an ink story is doing.

In the next section, we will follow a similar movement to what we did in the *Introducing procedural storytelling in ink* topic. In this first section, we focused on using multiple ink stories with the C# `Random` class while picking between them equally. However, most projects will want to only select ink stories based on preconditions. In the next section, we will look at conditionally choosing between ink stories.

Conditionally choosing stories

In the previous section, we saw how the C# Random class allows us to pick between objects based on the Story class as part of a collection, List<Story>. This has limited usefulness for most projects. Instead, most developers would prefer to have control over when an ink story is selected and the conditions under which it becomes available. In this section, we will look at a simple implementation of a system that checks the preconditions of a story before loading any of its contents. Values will be tracked across stories in the collection and, if the preconditions are met for the story, it will be considered available. If not, it will be ignored.

> **Note**
>
> The completed project for this section can be found in the *Chapter 12* examples on GitHub under the name Chapter12-ConditionalStories.
> Only select parts of the code will be shown as they relate to the concepts being examined.

To check the preconditions of ink stories, there needs to be a separate class, ConditionalStory, that contains the ink story and methods that originally appeared in the *Tracking quest values* subsection of the *Displaying and awarding player progression* section in *Chapter 11, Quest Tracking and Branching Narratives*, including simplified versions of ObserveVariables() and UpdateVariable():

```
public void ObserveVariables(Story.VariableObserver
   callback)
{
     InkStory.ObserveVariables(new List<string>() {
        "violence", "peace" }, callback);
}

public void UpdateVariable(string name, object value)
{
     if(InkStory.variablesState.
       GlobalVariableExistsWithName(name))
     {
         if (!InkStory.variablesState[name].Equals(value))
         {
             InkStory.variablesState[name] = value;
         }
     }
}
```

The `ConditionalStory` class has a method called `Available()`. Internally, this uses the `EvaluateFunction()` method of the `Story` class to call an ink function named `check()`. Assuming the ink story contains the function, it will be called, and the result will be converted into a Boolean value:

```
public bool Available()
{
    bool result = false;
    if(InkStory.HasFunction("check"))
    {
        result = (bool)
            InkStory.EvaluateFunction("check");
    }
    return result;
}
```

Each story file has a conditional check that is fed back into the `Available()` method of the `ConditionalStory` class. If the `check()` ink function returns `true`, the story is available for use.

Various changes have been made to the code shown in the previous section, *Using multiple stories*. The first is the use of `ConditionalStory` as a class containing an object based on the `Story` class. The second is the `SelectStories()` method. Unlike picking a random entry, it uses the `FindAll()` method of `List<ConditionalStory>` to search through its entries. If the `Available()` method, which is calling the `check()` ink function each time, reports `true`, it considers the story to be available:

```
List<ConditionalStory> selection = Stories.FindAll(e =>
    e.Available());

if (selection.Count > 0)
{
    System.Random rand = new System.Random();
    int index = rand.Next(selection.Count);
    ConditionalStory entry = selection[index];
    Stories.Remove(entry);
    UpdateContent(entry);
}
```

If each ink story defines how and if it is available for use in a larger project, this allows the ink and C# code in Unity to be developed separately. To become available so that it can be selected, the check() function in ink must report true to the ConditionalStory class in C#. This creates a simple but easily repeatable pattern for creating conditional stories in Unity based on understanding how its collections work by using the FindAll() method, as specified in this section, and the Random class, as specified in the previous section, in C# to access individual entries based on their indices.

Summary

The goal of this chapter was not to solve all problems with procedural storytelling or to cover every possible algorithm. The first topic, *Introducing procedural storytelling in ink*, reviewed the important concepts, such as how randomness can play a role in selecting content in ink. The second section, *Loading values into ink*, looked at how more advanced concepts such as grammars and story planning can be used with ink. Finally, in the *Coding collections in Unity* topic, we saw how Unity can be used to randomly select ink stories in a collection in the first section, as well as how some simple conditional testing can be incorporated by communicating between ink stories and C# classes in Unity.

We have now completed the last chapter of this book and hope that you will walk away with different concepts to explore and with simple patterns to use for much more advanced projects. Procedural storytelling is a diverse and deep subject. Many researchers and developers have created and continue to explore possible ways to build substitution grammars, plan for stories, and use ink and Unity, either separately or together, to craft simple rules for complex stories and experiences for players.

Questions

1. What is procedural storytelling?
2. What is a random table?
3. What is weighted randomness?
4. What is substitution grammar?
5. What is story planning?

Assessments

This section contains answers to questions from all the chapters.

Chapter 1 – Text, Flow, Choices, and Weaves

1. The story is the content, and the narrative is the experience of it. In nonlinear storytelling, the story is potentially experienced in a different order, with each reordering creating a new narrative for the reader.

2. ink understands flow as movement through the story as a narrative-like experience. In ink, this can "*run out*" when there are no paths to the end of the story.

3. Multiple lines can be combined using glue, a combination of less-than and greater-than symbols.

4. A weave is a collection of choices.

5. The different types of choices are basic, often called disappearing, and sticky choices. The first can only be used once and the second multiple times, as they "stick around" across weave usages.

6. Selective output allows an author to *select* what to use when shaping an option based on the text of the choice in ink. Different amounts of text can be shown to the reader based on the use of opening and closing square brackets with the text of the choice.

7. Sticky choices keep options open for later use. In more complex stories, the reader may return to a weave and pick a different or the same option again.

Chapter 2 – Knots, Diverts, and Looping Patterns

1. A knot is a section of a story with a name that can be diverted to ink.

2. DONE ends the current flow and END stops the story completely.

3. A stitch is a sub-section of a story that can only appear inside a knot.

4. The INCLUDE keyword pulls in other files and allows a project to use multiple files with their own knots and stitches available to the whole project.

5. A labeled option creates a value that is increased each time it is shown. Conditional values, on the other hand, allow for comparing variables and values. If the condition is true when used with an option, it will be shown. Otherwise, it will be hidden.

Chapter 3 – Sequences, Cycles, and Shuffling Text

1. The three types of alternatives are sequences, cycles, and shuffles.

2. The single-line forms of sequences, cycles, and shuffles all use the vertical bar, |, between elements.

3. The ampersand, &, is used before the first element as an alternative to creating a cycle.

4. A sequence will show each of the elements until the last. A cycle will loop back to the first element after its last one.

5. A shuffle picks a random element from its set each time it is run.

6. Multi-line sequences use the stopping keyword. This is unlike cycles and shuffles, which each use the name of the type of alternative as the keyword to create their multi-line forms.

Chapter 4 – Variables, Lists, and Functions

1. Assignment happens any time a variable is given a new value. This happens when a variable is first created in ink and can also happen on single lines of code.

2. A new string created based on two strings being added, or between a string and numerical value, is known as concatenation.

3. The tilde defines a single line of code in ink. It is often used with assignment, to call a function, or to perform some other single-line action.

4. The values in a list are part of a Boolean set. This means they are either true or false. In ink, all values in a list are set to false by default. To change to true, they must be surrounded by opening and closing parentheses.

5. The technical term for a variable defined as part of a function or a knot is a parameter. It affects the calculations or how content is processed by the function.

Chapter 5 – Tunnels and Threads

1. To create a tunnel, a divert must be used before and after the name of a knot or stitch. Within the knot or stitch, two diverts must be used together to return from the tunnel.

2. Tunnels connect two different locations in ink. They can be used between knots, stitches, or other locations in a story. Tunnels move the flow to a location and then return when two diverts are encountered.

3. A divert moves the flow to another knot or stitch. A tunnel uses two diverts to move to a knot or stitch and then returns to where it started. A thread is the inverse of a divert. It moves the knot or stitch to the current flow location instead of moving the flow to the knot or stitch.

4. Normally, multiple threads cannot be used on the same line. However, when using alternatives, it is possible to include multiple threads as part of the same structure. They are still accessed one at a time but can be grouped together on one line.

Chapter 6 – Adding and Working with the ink-Unity Integration Plugin

1. No, Inkle, the maintainers of the ink-Unity Integration plugin, do not recommend using the version found in the Unity Asset Store. This version is often out of date.

2. When the ink-Unity Integration plugin is installed in a project, new ink files can be created using the Create menu. This can be accessed using the **Project** window toolbar, right-clicking in the **Project** window, or via the **Assets** menu by selecting **Create**.

3. Inky is a good choice for editing ink source files. However, it needs to be associated with ink source files, which can be opened by double-clicking on files in the **Project** window.

4. Yes, the auto-compilation process can be adjusted by opening the **Project** Settings, selecting **Ink**, and then changing the **Compile All Ink Automatically** option.

Chapter 7 – Unity API – Making Choices and Story Progression

1. The Continue() method only loads a single line of ink text content and the next weave it encounters each time it is called. The ContinueMaximally() method loads all text content until it encounters a weave or the end of the story.

2. The `ChooseChoiceIndex()` method expects an `int` value within the range of the total number of entries in the `currentChoices` property in the `Story` class.

3. The `canContinue` property is a Boolean value. If there is more story content, it will be `true`. Otherwise, it will be `false`. The `canContinue` property should always be checked as part of a conditional statement before using the `Continue()` or `ContinueMaximally()` methods to prevent either method from throwing an error.

4. A prefab is a `GameObject` instance saved as an asset in Unity. Any game object used as part of the **Hierarchy** view can be saved as an asset by dragging it into the **Project** window. A copy of a prefab can be created during runtime through a process called *instantiation* in Unity.

5. For a weave encountered in a running ink story, the `currentChoices` properties will contain a `List<Choice>` instance, where each entry is an object based on the `Choice` class with `text` and `index` properties.

Chapter 8 – Story API – Accessing ink Variables and Functions

1. Yes, once a variable is created in ink, it can be accessed at any point in the story. By using the `variablesState` property as part of the Story API, the values of variables can also be accessed and changed.

2. Because functions are global in ink, this means they can be accessed from any point in an ink story. When working with the ink-Unity Integration plugin, the `HasFunction()` and `EvaluateFunction()` methods as part of the Story API provide the ability to test for a global function in an ink story and evaluate it, if it exists. The `EvaluateFunction()` method calls the ink function and can be used to pass data to ink or retrieve the text output of the function using the `out` C# keyword.

3. Unlike text content, the values of variables in ink exist outside of story progression controlled by the `Continue()` method or `ContinueMaximally()` method. However, because variables are global, their values can be changed during the action of loading a line or a larger chunk of a story. The value of a variable might be changed because of using either the `Continue()` method or `ContinueMaximally()` method, but they are not technically needed to work with variables in ink.

4. Any variables can be accessed by using their name in quotation marks within square brackets when working with the `variablesState` property as part of the Story API. While the same API provides methods for working with variables in ink, the shorthand syntax is often the preferred way to access and change the values of variables.

5. Yes. It is recommended to use the `HasFunction()` method for functions before attempting to change the value of a variable or evaluate a function. This will help prevent potentially game-crashing problems.

6. The `out` C# keyword provides a way to pass a variable by reference instead of passing only its value. This is an easy way to retrieve the text output of an ink function as a parameter to the `EvaluateFunction()` method of the Story API.

Chapter 9 – Story API – Observing and Reacting to Story Events

1. The `ObserveVariable()` and `ObserveVariables()` methods are based on the use of the action of *observing* variables. This separates the reaction in Unity from the action in ink. The action of observing allows Unity to react in any way it wants. The methods only provide the name of the variable and its new value.

2. Delegated functions are the second parameter of both the `ObserveVariable()` and `ObserveVariables()` methods. The use of the `delegate` C# keyword *delegates* the running of a function because of another function or method. The `ObserveVariable()` and `ObserveVariables()` methods are used in a callback approach.

3. The first, the `ObserveVariable()` method, accepts the name of a single variable and a delegated function to be called when it changes. The second, the `ObserveVariables()` method, accepts a `List<string>` instance of variables to watch and a delegated function. In both cases, the delegated function will be called with the name of the variable that changed and its new value.

4. The `variablesState` property provides direct access to ink variables and their current values by their names. However, the name of the ink variable must be used to access its value as part of recurring code such as might be found in the `Update()` or `FixedUpdate()` methods in Unity. The `ObserveVariable()` and `ObserveVariables()` methods allow a developer to write code that only runs when one or more ink variables change and only then. This can free up time each cycle to only run the necessary code and then update Unity when ink itself updates some value.

Chapter 10 – Dialogue Systems with ink

1. A hashtag is created when the hash (#) is used to create a tag on a single line in ink. Hashtags are used to add extra data per line.

2. A hashtag can only be used at the end of a line, but a speech tag is often used at the beginning of a line. A speech tag is always used to mark who is communicating, but a hashtag conveys extra information of any form.

3. The branching patterns of dialogue often look like trees, where the initial set of choices appears as a "*trunk*," with each branch moving outward into its own sets.

4. The list pattern presents options in a vertical arrangement. It can display multiple sentences per option but often needs scroll bars to present all the options within a set. It is best used when there is more visual spacing available for dialogue choices.

5. The radial menu pattern presents options clockwise on the screen. It is often used with video game consoles or other limited visual space contexts. Because of the reduced amount of spacing, options often appear as single words, icons, or short descriptions of their outcomes.

Chapter 11 – Quest Tracking and Branching Narratives

1. A quest is a series of events connected to a character within a story.

2. The name of the ink knot used to progress a quest is `progress`.

3. The `ChoosePathString()` method abruptly moves the current location from one section to another.

4. The global property in Unity is named `Application.dataPath`.

5. Polling requires checking values in one system from another. The events-based approach allows one system to observe another and respond to changes (events) as they happen.

Chapter 12 – Procedural Storytelling with ink

1. **Procedural storytelling** occurs when the story of a project is generated by procedures, or rules, that dynamically plan or shape content for a player.

2. A **random table** is a set of entries where individual values are chosen at random. Originally created as tables where rows were chosen using dice, the same concept can be used in ink with shuffles.

3. **Randomness** can be weighted toward certain probabilities. In ink, the RANDOM ( ) function can be used to decide the probability of entries instead of the default equal amounts when using the shuffle functionality.

4. A **grammar** is a set of rules for a language. A substitution grammar decides the substitution of words or phrases according to a set of rules. Often, substitution grammars are used with random entries or according to conditional rules.

5. **Story planning** is the ordering of story content based on rules. Story planning is based on using a substitution grammar for deciding which parts of a project a player might experience, either before play starts or because of certain player actions.

Packt.com

Subscribe to our online digital library for full access to over 7,000 books and videos, as well as industry leading tools to help you plan your personal development and advance your career. For more information, please visit our website.

Why subscribe?

- Spend less time learning and more time coding with practical eBooks and Videos from over 4,000 industry professionals

- Improve your learning with Skill Plans built especially for you

- Get a free eBook or video every month

- Fully searchable for easy access to vital information

- Copy and paste, print, and bookmark content

Did you know that Packt offers eBook versions of every book published, with PDF and ePub files available? You can upgrade to the eBook version at packt.com and as a print book customer, you are entitled to a discount on the eBook copy. Get in touch with us at customercare@packtpub.com for more details.

At www.packt.com, you can also read a collection of free technical articles, sign up for a range of free newsletters, and receive exclusive discounts and offers on Packt books and eBooks.

Other Books You May Enjoy

If you enjoyed this book, you may be interested in these other books by Packt:

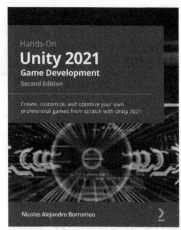

Hands-On Unity 2021 Game Development - Second Edition

Nicolas Alejandro Borromeo

ISBN: 9781801071482

- Explore both C# and Visual Scripting tools to customize various aspects of a game, such as physics, gameplay, and the UI

- Program rich shaders and effects using Unity's new Shader Graph and Universal Render Pipeline

- Implement postprocessing to improve graphics quality with full-screen effects

- Create rich particle systems for your Unity games from scratch using VFX Graph and Shuriken

- Add animations to your game using the Animator, Cinemachine, and Timeline

- Use the brand-new UI Toolkit package to create user interfaces

- Implement game AI to control character behavior

Game Development Patterns with Unity 2021 - Second Edition

David Baron

ISBN: 9781800200814

- Structure professional Unity code using industry-standard development patterns
- Identify the right patterns for implementing specific game mechanics or features
- Develop configurable core game mechanics and ingredients that can be modified without writing a single line of code
- Review practical object-oriented programming (OOP) techniques and learn how they're used in the context of a Unity project
- Build unique game development systems such as a level editor
- Explore ways to adapt traditional design patterns for use with the Unity API

Packt is searching for authors like you

If you're interested in becoming an author for Packt, please visit `authors.packtpub.com` and apply today. We have worked with thousands of developers and tech professionals, just like you, to help them share their insight with the global tech community. You can make a general application, apply for a specific hot topic that we are recruiting an author for, or submit your own idea.

Share Your Thoughts

Now you've finished *Dynamic Story Scripting with the ink Scripting Language*, we'd love to hear your thoughts! Scan the QR code below to go straight to the Amazon review page for this book and share your feedback or leave a review on the site that you purchased it from.

https://packt.link/r/1-801-81932-7

Your review is important to us and the tech community and will help us make sure we're delivering excellent quality content.

Index